Clergy in the Classroom:

The Religion of Secular Humanism

Second Edition

David A. Noebel

J.F. Baldwin & Kevin J. Bywater

Summit Press

Manitou Springs, Colorado 80829

Summit Press
P.O. Box 207
Manitou Springs, CO 80829
(719) 685-9103
www.summit.org

Clergy in the Classroom: The Religion of Secular Humanism, Second Edition
David A. Noebel, J.F. Baldwin, and Kevin J. Bywater

First edition, 1995
Second edition, 2001

ISBN 0-936163-28-3 (paperback)
ISBN 0-936163-29-1 (hardback)

Cover Design by Jeff Stoddard

Table of Contents

THE CASE PRESENTED

Many people view Secular Humanism as mere fiction — a construct of the "religious right."[1] It is asserted that Secular Humanism is the new "bogeyman" for religious conservatives — a phantom suspected around every corner, in every classroom, and over every courtroom. But a denial of the reality of Secular Humanism is simply naïve, an attitude founded more in fantasy than the facts.

The Reality of Secular Humanism

To find the facts, one need not look all that far. Humanists are quite open about their belief system and their goals. Books such as the *Humanist Manifestos I,II, and 2000* and publications like *Free Inquiry* and *The Humanist* openly proclaim the Humanist worldview and agenda. Indeed, the Secular Humanist worldview is described comprehensively in David A. Noebel's 912-page textbook, *Understanding the Times: The Religious Worldviews of Our Day and the Search for Truth.*[2]

Even a precursory examination of the evidence makes it clear that Secular Humanism is a real worldview adhered to and propagated by many intellectuals and leaders in the 20th century. What is also evident, and more startling, is that Secular Humanism is a religion — and the only worldview granted privileged access to our government-sponsored public schools. Until now, the proof that Secular Humanism is a religion has not been organized into an easily-accessible format. This book, the culmination of more than 20 years of research, contains arguments and assertions by dozens of Humanists (many of them leaders) that permit only one conclusion: The "wall of separation" between church and state has effectively established Secular Humanism as the official religion of America's public schools. How did this happen?

The Growth of Secularism

How did America move from its founding as a Christian nation to what Francis A. Schaeffer refers to as the "post-Christian" era? According to Nancy Pearcey and Charles Thaxton, this cultural shift toward secularism began in England. They write,

> In late nineteenth-century England, several small groups of scientists and scholars organized under the leadership of Thomas H. Huxley to overthrow the cultural dominance of Christianity — particularly the intellectual dominance of the Anglican church. Their goal was to secularize society, replacing the Christian worldview with scientific naturalism, a worldview that recognizes the existence of nature alone. Though secularists, they understood very well that they were replacing one religion by another, for they described their goal as the establishment of the 'church scientific.' Huxley even referred to his scientific lectures as 'lay sermons.'[3]

As this cultural shift gained momentum in England, it was exported to America. During the same time, the American educational establishment was gradually turning its back on Christianity,[4] and the left-wing Unitarian church began preaching secularism in the form of *Humanist Sermons* and *Humanist Religion* (see Exhibits 6 and 7) .[5]

The tide of anti-Christian sentiment has swelled in recent times.

"The secularist camp," says James Davison Hunter, "[now] represents the fastest growing community of 'moral conviction' in America."[6] Hunter estimates that adherents to a humanistic perspective comprise 11 percent of the population of the United States,[7] though not all of these individuals are members of Humanist organizations. Indeed, a person need not label himself or herself a Humanist in order to adhere to the basic components of the Humanist worldview.

Hunter's observation is by no means singular. He notes that most scholars "recognize the secular character of public life and the fact that there is a growing constituency who favor these circumstances." Writes Hunter:

> Based on mountains of empirical evidence, drawing from the work of Max Weber, Emile Durkheim, and Robert Bellah, one could argue quite plausibly that secular humanism has become the dominant moral ideology of American public culture and now plays much the same role as the pan-Protestant ideology played in the nineteenth century.[8]

Secular Humanism: A religion (worldview) which promotes theological atheism, philosophical naturalism, biological spontaneous generation/ evolution, moral relativism, legal positivism, and political globalism.

The "pan-Protestant ideology" Hunter refers to was the common vision of many educational leaders in the nineteenth century. Their goal was to establish a common school system that transcended the distinctives of Protestant denominations, but where the Bible could still be read, recited and recommended. Roman Catholic leaders, notes George Marsden, protested the "Protestant efforts to impose a single educational system."

> Catholics not only objected to such practices as the reading of the Protestant version of the Bible or reciting the Ten Commandments in Protestant form but also, more substantially, to the idea that the Bible "could speak for itself." Catholic doctrine said just the opposite. The Bible was to be understood under the guidance of the church

3

authority. The idea that children should "judge for themselves" was not neutral, as it sounded, but a sectarian Protestant doctrine.[9]

The concern in our day is no longer with regard to a generic Protestantism (which was little more than Unitarianism in reality). In our day, a state-sponsored and defended *secular* perspective is offered as "neutral," promoting neither a Protestant nor a Roman Catholic perspective. Contained in this secular perspective are all the basic elements of the Secular Humanist worldview. Indeed, the practices negated by Secular Humanism are negated in our public schools. For example, in contrast to traditional religions such as Judaism, Christianity and Islam, Secular Humanists do not pray. The negation of prayer is the default practice of the common schools of our day. This is far from neutral; it is *practical atheism*. How could a practical atheism ever be neutral?

The nineteenth century Catholic leaders found it necessary to establish their own private schools — lest their children be instructed in a non-neutral, generic Protestantism. In the same way, many Evangelical Christians today find it imperative to establish private schools or initiate homeschooling in order to avoid the indoctrination of their children in a non-neutral, generic Humanism promoted and practiced in the public schools.

> "So, in public schools we strain out the gnat of graduation prayer and swallow the camel of quasi-secular religion in the curriculum."
> —Ralph Gillman
> Letter to the Editor,
> *First Things*, October 2000, p. 11

Tragically, this Humanism has even influenced many modern mainline Christian churches. As Hunter notes, one of the primary differences between traditional/orthodox wings of religious traditions and liberal/progressive wings is that "liberal religious traditions share much more in common culturally with one another and with the growing secularist population than they do with those orthodox believers in their own religious heritage."[10]

As secularism gradually has gained great influence over American culture,[11] the champions of Secular Humanism have almost unanimously

4

described themselves as promoters of a new religion — a religion more highly evolved than "the rotting corpse of Christianity" (Exhibit 32).[12]

Can we take them at their word? Is Secular Humanism a religion? Is it realistic to define "religion" in a way that includes the Secular Humanist worldview?

What Is Religion?

If "religion" is defined narrowly, as that which posits a transcendent deity, then Secular Humanism is not a religion. But if "religion" is defined in a way that includes non-theistic worldviews like Buddhism or Confucianism, then it certainly applies to Secular Humanism.

Defining "religion" is no easy task. To succeed, one must provide a definition that properly includes well-known religious traditions (such as Buddhism, Judaism, or Mormonism), and yet excludes those social realities which are not authentically religious (such as health-driven vegetarian diets, over-zealous sports fans, and political parties). The latter may ape religion in fervency, thus functioning in a quasi-religious form; nevertheless, they fail to develop in terms of full-fledged *worldviews*.

There are two basic approaches to defining "religion": the *substantive* approach, which focuses on the content of the belief system, and the *functional* approach, which focuses on what the belief system does for the individual or community. Hunter explains:

> "One must provide a definition that properly includes well-known religious traditions (such as Buddhism, Judaism, or Mormonism), and yet excludes those social realities which are not authentically religious (such as health-driven vegetarian diets, over-zealous sports fans, and political parties)."

The substantive model generally delimits religion to the range of traditional theisms: Judaism, Christianity, Islam, Hinduism, and so on. The functional model, in contrast, is more inclusive. By defining religion according to its social function, the functional model treats religion largely as synonymous with such terms as cultural system, belief system, meaning system, moral order, ideology, world view, and cosmology.[13]

The fatal flaw of most substantive definitions is their insistence that a belief in the divine is essential to religion. Of course, such approaches miscarry in that they fail to encompass the realities of non-theistic religions such as Confucianism. Thus, even though it is appropriate to employ a substantive definition of religion, it is clear that we must avoid a default inclusion of the divine.

One promising proposal defines "religion" as "a set of beliefs, actions, and emotions, both personal and corporate, organized around the concept of an Ultimate Reality. This Reality may be understood as a unity or a plurality, personal or nonpersonal, divine or not, and so forth, differing from religion to religion."[14] Such a definition adequately encompasses both theistic and non-theistic worldview traditions. It also avoids inclusion of non-religious social realities such as sports team advocacy and political parties, neither of which properly makes reference to an "Ultimate Reality." Of course, such a definition clearly encompasses Secular Humanism.

Religion and the Courts

As America has moved toward secularism, her courts have gradually accepted less restrictive understandings of religion. The U.S. Supreme Court has progressed from a *substantive* understanding toward a *functional* understanding.[15] In the 19th century, the Supreme Court understood "religion" in terms of traditional religions. In *Davis v. Beason* (1890), for example, the Court ruled against the teaching and practice of polygamy (declaring both to be criminal actions), on the basis of "the general consent of the Christian world in modern times."[16] Also, in *Church of the Holy Trinity v. United States* (1892) Justice David Brewer stated in the majority decision, "this is a Christian nation."[17]

In the 20th century, a broader understanding of religion — one that would include non-Christian and non-theistic religions — has emerged.

In *United States v. Kauten* (2d Cir. 1943), conscientious objector status was granted to Mathias Kauten, not on the basis of his belief in God, but on the basis of his "religious conscience." The court concluded: "Conscientious objection may justly be regarded as a response of the individual to an inward mentor, call it conscience or God, that is for many persons at the present time the equivalent of what has always been thought a religious impulse."[18] Thus, the Court adopted a functional understanding of religion, as opposed to a distinctly theistic one.

Another example of the Court's adoption of a functional understanding of religion occurred in *Fellowship of Humanity v. County of Alameda* (1957).[19] In this case, the Fellowship of Humanity sought recovery of property taxes because, it argued, its grounds were used for religious worship. They were awarded a refund of paid property taxes. Other cases awarding religious tax-exemption to non-theistic bodies involved the Washington Ethical Society and the Fellowship of Reconciliation. Paul Blanshard, a signatory of the *Humanist Manifesto II*, declared that the Fellowship of Humanity court decision represented "another victory for those who would interpret the word 'religion' very broadly. . ." (Exhibit 25).[20]

> "Among religions in this country which do not teach what would generally be considered a belief in the existence of God are Buddhism, Taoism, Ethical Culture, Secular Humanism, and others."
> —U.S. Supreme Court
> *Torcaso v. Watkins* (1961)

Another example of the court's use of a functional definition of religion is well-known. In 1961 the Supreme Court handed down the *Torcaso v. Watkins* decision regarding a Maryland notary public who was initially disqualified from office because he would not declare a belief in God. But the Court ruled in his favor. It argued that theistic religions could not be favored by the Court over non-theistic religions. In a footnote it clarified what it meant by non-theistic religions: "Among religions in this country which do not teach what would generally be considered a belief in the existence of God are Buddhism, Taoism, Ethical Culture, Secular Humanism, and others" (Exhibit 26).[21]

Clearly, the Supreme Court's understanding of religion has broadened enough to include non-theistic religions like Buddhism and Secular Humanism. Unfortunately, the Court has not been consistent in applying this understanding to its present interpretation of the First Amendment. If the no-establishment clause of the First Amendment really means that there should be a "wall of separation" between church and state, why are only theistic religions disestablished? If Secular Humanism is a religion — something the U.S. Supreme Court has claimed, and something countless Humanists proclaim (as seen throughout the Exhibits that follow) — why is it allowed access to our public schools when there is to be no established religion? As Hunter observes,

> "Education is thus a most powerful ally of Humanism, and every American public school is a school of Humanism. What can the theistic Sunday-schools, meeting for an hour once a week, and teaching only a fraction of the children, do to stem the tide of a five-day program of humanistic teaching?"
> — Charles Francis Potter,
> *Humanism: A New Religion*

To be legally consistent the courts will either have to articulate a constitutional double standard or apply the functional definition of religion to the no establishment clause just as they have to the free exercise [clause]. The latter would mean that secularistic faiths and ideologies would be rigorously prohibited from receiving even indirect support from the state, which — needless to say — would have enormous implications for public education.[22]

Secular Humanism and Public Education

As soon as secularism gained a foothold in American culture, Humanists began using public education to proselytize the next generation. In 1930, *Humanist Manifesto I* signatory Charles Francis Potter boldly declared that "Education is thus a most powerful ally of Humanism, and every American public school is a school of Humanism. What can the theistic Sunday-schools, meeting for an hour once a week, and teaching only a fraction of the children, do to stem the tide of a five-day program of humanistic teaching?" (Exhibit 9).[23] As one would expect, this Humanistic "program" is extremely intolerant of any theistic religions.

Why are Christianity and other theistic religions banned from the public schools while the religion of Secular Humanism is granted easy access to the classroom? The only explanation yet offered is that Humanism is a neutral and tolerant perspective. Nothing could be further from the truth! Humanists in the public schools have consistently attacked the Christian worldview, with some even going so far as attempting to erase traces of Christian influence on history, science, and other disciplines (Exhibit 37).[24]

Further, Humanists preach a faith every bit as dogmatic as Christianity. Moral relativism is foundational for Secular Humanist ethics; spontaneous generation and evolution are basic to their biology; naturalism is foundational to their philosophy; and atheism is their theological perspective (see Exhibits 12, 20, 28, 40).

The Case of Paul Kurtz and *Eupraxophy*

Recently, some Humanists have recognized that if their worldview is religious, it has no more right than any other religion (under the present interpretation of the First Amendment) to be sanctioned by the American government and promoted in public schools as a neutral perspective. Paul Kurtz (editor of *Free Inquiry* and publisher of Prometheus Books) is the most aggressive Humanist to take up the task of redefining Humanism as non-religious. In his book, *Eupraxophy: Living Without Religion*, he argues that Secular Humanism, while not a neutral worldview, is also not a religion. Humanists who claim otherwise are simply mistaken.[25]

Dr. Kurtz has not always held this view. He writes,

> At one time I was persuaded to extend the term *religious* to incorporate a wide range of humanist beliefs and practices, for I noted the passionate commitment that humanism could arouse. If nothing

> "At one time, I was persuaded to extend the term *religious* to incorporate a wide range of humanist beliefs and practices. . . [I]t seemed to me then to have been a wise strategy for the humanist movement. . ."
> — Paul Kurtz, *Eupraxophy: Living Without Religion*

9

else, it seemed to me then to have been a wise strategy for the humanist movement to adopt, that is, to consider itself a religion of the future.[26]

A "wise strategy" indeed. If one wants the privileges adherents of traditional religions enjoy — such as tax-exemption and conscientious objector status, then gaining recognition as a religion is certainly effective. As Kurtz notes, "liberal religious humanists had previously argued, against the steadfast opposition of theists, that a belief system without God functioned religiously and was entitled to all the exemptions and privileges that theistic religions enjoyed." These Humanists won court cases (Exhibits 25 and 26) and gained social status. Their reasoning was so effective that "many conservative theistic critics of humanism now accept the earlier claim of some humanists that humanism is a religion."[27]

This would seem like good news. The Humanists made their case. The conclusion? Their worldview is just as religious as any other. On this there was finally agreement. But as the political tide turned, and Court rulings restricted religious expression and advocacy in the public realm, especially in the public schools, Kurtz changed his "strategy."

Today we are confronted with a new challenge, for conservative theists not only say they agree with this claim [that Humanism is a religion] but go further: Even *secular* humanism, they insist, is a "religion," and as such it must be bound by all the limits placed on theistic religions in democratic societies. This argument is particularly cutting in the American context, for the First Amendment to the United States Constitution explicitly forbids the establishment of a religion. The critics of humanism maintain that there has been a de facto establishment of secular humanism in the modern world, especially in the public schools and the judicial system. If secular humanism is a religion, they insist, then it has no right to a privileged place; for example, it cannot be taught to the young, using public funds and in the guise of neutrality.[28]

10

As has been seen, Dr. Kurtz is well aware of the stakes, as his new strategy reveals. Even so, it is not without its flaws and fallacies. For example, while he attempts to redefine Secular Humanism as non-religious, he fails to provide a definition of religion that includes religious traditions which are non-theistic, while at the same time excluding Secular Humanism. Nevertheless, he attempts his case along several lines.

First, Kurtz denies that Secular Humanism has "certain of the essential characteristics of a religion. In particular, humanism does not assert a god or other sacred realities, nor does it carry with it the distinctive symbols or functions of traditional religions."[29] His line of reasoning is flawed. Being non-theistic does not disqualify a worldview as being religious. Buddhism, Confucianism, and Taoism are non-theistic. Who would deny their status as bona fide religions?

In addition, Secular Humanism does engage in religious functions and offer a common symbolism. Secular Humanist clergy perform weddings, funerals, naming ceremonies, and the like — functions often performed by religions (Exhibits 45, 46, 48, 51). Indeed, there are Humanist Churches, complete with skits, songs, and brief messages of challenge and encouragement (Exhibit 52). And with regards to meaningful symbols, the "Darwin Fish" provides a visual identifier every bit as effective as the Christian Ichthys symbol or the Masonic Square and Compass.

Second, Kurtz supplies his own understanding of religion: "the distinctive force of the term *religion* involves some belief *in a divine or sacred reality and some binding relationship of worship or devotion to it*." Needless to say, strategizes Kurtz, "Under this definition, humanism is excluded from the rubric" (54). But as he discusses Confucianism and Buddhism he is quizzed:

An interesting question, indeed, is whether the terms *religion* and *philosophy* can even be applied to all the varieties of "religion" we encounter in the world. Buddhism, Hinduism, Taoism, and Confucianism do not fit Western conceptions of religion. Asian systems are unique

11

and there are so many divergences that even the term *philosophy* may not apply to them, even though Western writers have attempted to stretch the terms *religion* and *philosophy* to cover them. (64)

Kurtz is hard pressed to include Asian religions in *his* definition of religion. This is because his target is Western religions, as he admits: "My definition of religion applies especially to Christianity, Judaism, and Islam, the three great monotheistic religions; and it also applies to innumberable sects, denominations, and cults that have sprung up. But does this definition apply to other Asian religions?" (66). And here is where Kurtz admits his failure.

> Our discussion of Buddhism shows that it is difficult to find a common unitary thread underlying all religions; for some forms of Buddhism, such as Zen . . . the emphasis is on personal self-realization and enlightenment. Buddhism thus expresses a kind of eupraxia or life stance, focusing as it does on right conduct as the source of peace. It seeks to cultivate a style of life in order to achieve a state of release. Some Western thinkers have been attracted to Buddhism insofar as it is devoid of the mythology of a supernatural, miraculous religion and the doctrine of salvation by grace, but especially since it focuses on achieving moral equanimity in this life. (70-71)

Thus, Kurtz cannot supply a definition of religion that excludes Secular Humanism while including Buddhism. Yet Buddhism is universally recognized as a religion.

A third argument offered by Kurtz is one he considers to be "the Achilles heel" of the opposing view.

> The Achilles heel of this argument [that Humanism is a religion] is that it is theistic religions that have transformed themselves historically by assuming all-encompassing nonreligious moral, psychologicial, and sociological functions. The fact that religions may share these functions with other human interests and institutions does not make these other interests and institutions religious.[30]

12

So, Kurtz casts theistic religions with a "Johnny-come-lately" façade. While many scholars have asserted an evolutionary character to religions, Kurtz's view is distinctly eccentric. Never does Kurtz justify his peculiar claim that religions have "tranformed themselves" into "all-encompassing nonreligious moral, psychological, and sociological functions." Besides, what could he mean when he asserts that theistic religions have adopted "nonreligious" elements? Students of history, especially the history of religions, recognize that religions naturally provide all-encompassing perspectives — that is the nature of worldviews.[31]

Fourth, Kurtz rejects the label "religion" as applied to Secular Humanism and offers a new term: "Eupraxophy."

I have come up with the term *eupraxophy*, which means "good practical wisdom." *Eupraxophy* is derived from the following [Greek] roots: *eu-*, *praxis*, and *sophia*. *Eu-* is a prefix which means "good," "well," "advantageous". . . *Praxis* (or *prassein*) refers to "action, doing, or practice." *Eupraxia* means "right action" or "good conduct." The suffix *sophia* is derived from *sophos* ("wise") and means "wisdom."[32]

> "It would be more difficult to use the term religion to describe humanism if humanists rejected it consistently, but the majority do not."
> — James Davison Hunter, "Religious Freedom and the Challenge of Modern Pluralism"

Lest one infer that a *eupraxophy* is a neutral perspective, Kurtz explains why it is not. It is no mere philosophy. It is not simply science. It is neither simple atheism nor mere humanistic sentimentalism. Rather a *eupraxophy* is a distinct and well-developed worldview. As Kurtz asserts,

[E]upraxophy moves beyond philosophy and science in seeking to present a coherent life view as the basis upon which we are willing to act. It is the ground upon which we stand, the ultimate outlook that controls our view of reality. Accordingly the primary task of eupraxophy is to understand nature and life and to draw concrete normative prescriptions from this knowledge. . . It involves at least a double focus: a cosmic perspective and a set of normative ideals by which we may live.[33]

As a "eupraxophy," Secular Humanism is analogous to Buddhism, as Kurtz admits: "Buddhism thus expresses a kind of eupraxia or life stance, focusing as it does on right conduct as the source of peace" (71). Nevertheless, regardless of Kurtz's resistance to include Buddhism as a religion, the consensus among scholars is that it is a religion.

Secular Humanism is a non-neutral perspective, complete with a philosophical view of ultimate reality (metaphysical naturalism) and a set of normative ethical ideals. In short, it is a distinct and particular worldview. As such, it is neither *merely* scientific, nor *merely* philosophical. It is not derived in some generic way from microscopes and telescopes. Rather, it is firmly grounded in philosophical naturalism, non-theism, evolutionary theory, ethical relativism, and political globalism. In addition, it has clergy members, social ceremonies, and a developing symbolism (Exhibits 49, 53). This is the religion of Secular Humanism.

So, on what grounds should Kurtz's worldview be granted privileged access to public schools?

Summary

Secular Humanism is a real worldview. It has thrived in our newly secularized culture. And Secular Humanism is a religion, Kurtz's protests notwithstanding. His arguments to the contrary are unsuccessful. He is unable to provide a definition of religion that excludes Secular Humanism but includes other non-theistic religions. He offers a neologism, *eupraxophy*, in place of "religion"; but this is idiosyncratic and contradicts the arguments and assertions of almost every other Humanist leader or spokesperson. As Hunter notes, "It would be more difficult to use the term religion to describe humanism if humanists rejected it consistently, but the majority do not."[34] Finally, he admits that Secular Humanism is neither simple science nor neutral. And yet he still wants privileged access in our educational institutions, and our children

This work, *Clergy in the Classroom: The Religion of Secular Humanism*, provides exhibit after exhibit and testimony after testimony that combine into a crushing weight of evidence contrary to Kurtz. Secular Humanism, as we will see, is indisputably religious. The evidence leaves only one question unanswered — a rhetorical question so plaintive that it haunts the reader: Why is the United States government allowing the next generation of youth to be indoctrinated by Humanist clergy in the classroom?

NOTES

1. See, for example, David Bollier, "The Witch Hunt Against 'Secular Humanism,'" in *The Humanist* (September/October 1984), 11-19.
2. David A. Noebel, *Understanding the Times: The Religious Worldviews of Our Day and the Search for Truth* (Eugene, OR: Harvest House, 1991). Available from Summit Ministries (www.summit.org) or your local Christian bookstore.
3. Nancy R. Pearcey and Charles B. Thaxton, *The Soul of Science: Christian Faith and Natural Philosophy* (Wheaton, IL: Crossway Books, 1994), 19.
4. See George M. Marsden, *The Soul of the American University: From Protestant Establishment to Established Nonbelief* (New York: Oxford University Press, 1994).
5. *Humanist Sermons*, Curtis W. Reese, ed. (Chicago: Open Court, 1927); *Humanist Religion*, Curtis W. Reese (New York: The Macmillan Co., 1931).
6. James Davison Hunter, "Religious Freedom and the Challenge of Modern Pluralism," in *Articles of Faith, Articles of Peace: The Religious Liberty Clauses and the American Public Philosophy*, James Davison Hunter and Os Guiness, eds. (Washington, D.C.: The Bookings Institution, 1990), 57.
7. Isaac Asimov, then president of the American Humanist Association, said in a July 1989 letter to the membership of the AHA, "I estimate there are 7.3 million of us [humanists] right here in America."
8. Hunter, "Religious Freedom," 57.
9. Marsden, *The Soul of the American University*, 87-88.
10. Hunter, "Religious Freedom," 57.
11. See James C. Dobson and Gary L. Bauer, *Children at Risk: The Battle for the Hearts and Minds of Our Kids* (Dallas, TX: Word Publishing, 1990), 22: "The humanistic system of values has now become the predominant way of thinking in most of the power centers of society. It has outstripped the Judeo-Christian precepts in the universities, in the news media, in the entertainment industry, in the judiciary, in the federal bureaucracy, in business, medicine, law, psychology, sociology, in the arts, in many public schools, and, to be sure, in the halls of congress."
12. John H. Dunphy, "Public Education," *The Humanist* (January/February 1983), 26.
13. Hunter, "Religious Freedom," 58.
14. Michael Peterson, William Hasker, Bruce Reichenbach, and David Basinger, *Reason and Religious Belief: An Introduction to the Philosophy of Religion* (New York: Oxford University Press, 1991), 4. Italics removed from the original.

15. See the discussion in Hunter, "Religious Freedom," 59-62. See also John W. Whitehead and John B. Conlan, "The Establishment of the Religion of Secular Humanism and Its First Amendment Implications," in *Texas Tech Law Review* 10, no. 1 (1978): 1-66; and John W. Whitehead, *The Second American Revolution* (Wheaton: Crossway Books, 1982), chapter 9.
16. *Davis v. Beason*, 133 U.S. 333, 343 (1890).
17. *Church of the Holy Trinity v. United States*, 143 U.S. 457, 471 (1892). Cf. David A. Brewer, *The United States: A Christian Nation* (Philadelphia: The John D. Winston Company, 1905; reprinted Smyrna, GA: American Vision, Inc., 1996).
18. *United States v. Kauten*, 133F. 2nd 703, 708 (2d Cir. 1943). See also *United States v. Seeger*, 380 U.S. 163 (1965), where the court adopted Paul Tillich's understanding of religion to justify its use of the functional definition of religion.
19. *Fellowship of Humanity v. County of Alameda*, 153 Cal. App. 2nd. 673.
20. "Paul Blanshard's Column," in *The Humanist*, No.4, 1959, 238.
21. *Torcaso v. Watkins*, 367 U.S. 488, 495, fn. 11 (1961).
22. Hunter, "Religious Freedom," 72.
23. Charles Francis Potter, *Humanism: A New Religion* (New York: Simon and Schuster, 1930), 128.
24. See Paul C. Vitz, *Censorship: Evidence of Bias in Our Children's Textbooks* (Ann Arbor: Servant Books, 1986).
25. Paul Kurtz, *Eupraxophy: Living Without Religion* (Buffalo, NY: Prometheus Books, 1989).
26. Ibid., 11.
27. Ibid., 9.
28. Ibid., 9-10.
29. Ibid., 8.
30. Ibid., 12.
31. On the all-encompassing nature of religions, see, John F. Wilson, *Religion: A Preface* (Englewood Cliffs, NJ: Prentice-Hall, 1982); Ninian Smart, *The World's Religions*, 2nd Ed. (Cambridge: Cambridge University Press, 1989, 1998); *idem.*, *Worldviews: Crosscultural Explorations of Human Beliefs*, 2nd Ed. (Englewood Cliffs, NJ: Prentice Hall, 1995); Paul G. Heibert, R. Daniel Shaw, and Tite Tiénou, *Understanding Folk Religion* (Grand Rapids, MI: Baker Books, 1999). On the all-encompassing nature of worldviews, as well as worldviews as synonymous with religions, see, David A. Noebel, *Understanding the Times: The Religious Worldviews of Our Day and the Search for Truth* (Eugene, OR: Harvest House, 1991); James W. Sire, *The Universe Next Door: A Basic Worldview Catalog*, 3rd Ed. (Downers Grove, IL: InterVarsity Press, 1976, 1988, 1997); Ronald H. Nash, *Worldviews in Conflict: Choosing Christianity in a World of Ideas* (Grand Rapids, MI: Zondervan, 1992); *idem.*, *Life's Ultimate Questions: An Introduction to Philosophy* (Grand Rapids, MI: Zondervan, 1999).
32. Kurtz, *Eupraxophy*, 14.
33. Ibid., 19-20.
34. Hunter, "Religious Freedom," 65.

The Exhibits

The following exhibits have been reproduced in Adobe®
PageMaker®. They are *not* photocopies. Though they have been
altered to fit the layout of this book, they have not been materially
changed.

To owners of this book, the publisher hereby grants permission to
make overhead transparencies from the following exhibits.

Exhibit 1

1897

EDUCATION TODAY

By JOHN DEWEY

Edited and with a Foreword by

JOSEPH RATNER

What the best and wisest parent wants for his own child, that must the community want for all its children. Any other ideal for our schools is narrow and unlovely; acted upon it destroys our democracy.—JOHN DEWEY

G . P . PUTNAM'S SONS . *New York*

> " I believe that . . . education is the fundamental method of social progress and reform. "

MY PEDAGOGIC CREED   15

beautiful, the emotions will for the most part take care of themselves.

—next to deadness and dullness, formalism and routine, our education is threatened with no greater evil than sentimentalism.

—this sentimentalism is the necessary result of the attempt to divorce feeling from action.

Article V—*The School and Social Progress*

I Believe that

—education is the fundamental method of social progress and reform.

—all reforms which rest simply upon the enactment of law, or the threatening of certain penalties, or upon changes in mechanical or outward arrangements, are transitory and futile.

—education is a regulation of the process of coming to share in the social consciousness; and that the adjustment of individual activity on the basis of this social consciousness is the only sure method of social reconstruction.

—this conception has due regard for both the individualistic and social ideals. It is duly individual because it recognizes the formation of a certain character as the only genuine basis of right living. It is socialistic because it recognizes that this right character is not to be formed by merely individual precept, example, or exhortation, but rather by the influence of a certain form of institutional or community life upon the

This exhibit demonstrates that *Humanist Manifesto I* signatory John Dewey, the father of modern public education, believed that education and religion mix. These pages come from Dewey's "Pedagogic Creed" (originally published in 1897), and are here taken from the 1940 anthology of Dewey's articles and essays, *Education Today*, copyrighted by Dewey.

> **I believe that . . . it is the business of every one interested in education to insist upon the school as the primary and most effective instrument of social progress and reform. . . .**

individual, and that the social organism through the school, as its organ, may determine ethical results.

—in the ideal school we have the reconciliation of the individualistic and the institutional ideals.

—the community's duty to education is, therefore, its paramount moral duty. By law and punishment, by social agitation and discussion, society can regulate and form itself in a more or less haphazard and chance way. But through education society can formulate its own purposes, can organize its own means and resources, and thus shape itself with definiteness and economy in the direction in which it wishes to move.

—when society once recognizes the possibilities in this direction, and the obligations which these possibilities impose, it is impossible to conceive of the resources of time, attention, and money which will be put at the disposal of the educator.

—it is the business of every one interested in education to insist upon the school as the primary and most effective instrument of social progress and reform in order that society may be awakened to realize what the school stands for, and aroused to the necessity of endowing the educator with sufficient equipment properly to perform his task.

—education thus conceived marks the most perfect and intimate union of science and art conceivable in human experience.

—the art of thus giving shape to human powers and adapting them to social service is the supreme art; one calling into its service the best of artists; that no insight,

sympathy, tact, executive power, is too great for such service.

—with the growth of psychological service, giving added insight into individual structure and laws of growth; and with growth of social science, adding to our knowledge of the right organization of individuals, all scientific resources can be utilized for the purposes of education.

—when science and art thus join hands the most commanding motive for human action will be reached, the most genuine springs of human conduct aroused, and the best service that human nature is capable of guaranteed.

—the teacher is engaged, not simply in the training of individuals, but in the formation of the proper social life.

—every teacher should realize the dignity of his calling; that he is a social servant set apart for the maintenance of proper social order and the securing of the right social growth.

—in this way the teacher always is the prophet of the true God and the usherer in of the true kingdom of God.

> **I believe that . . . in this way the teacher is the prophet of the true God and the usherer in of the true kingdom of God.**

Exhibit 2

1908

EDUCATION TODAY

By JOHN DEWEY

Edited and with a Foreword by

JOSEPH RATNER

What the best and wisest parent wants for his own child, that must the community want for all its children. Any other ideal for our schools is narrow and unlovely; acted upon it destroys our democracy.—JOHN DEWEY

G . P . PUTNAM'S SONS . *New York*

> **" "Our schools . . . are performing an infinitely significant religious work." "**

84   EDUCATION TODAY

This question of the mode, time, and stuff of specific instruction trenches indeed upon a question in which national temper and tradition count for much. We do not find it feasible or desirable to put upon the regular teachers the burden of teaching a subject which has the nature of religion. The alternative plan of parceling out pupils among religious teachers drawn from their respective churches and denominations brings us up against exactly the matter which has done most to discredit the churches, and to discredit the cause, not perhaps of religion, but of organized and institutional religion: the multiplication of rival and competing religious bodies, each with its private inspiration and outlook. Our schools, in bringing together those of different nationalities, languages, traditions, and creeds, in assimilating them together upon the basis of what is common and public in endeavor and achievement, are performing an infinitely significant religious work. They are promoting the social unity out of which in the end genuine religious unity must grow. Shall we interfere with this work? Shall we run the risk of undoing it by introducing into education a subject which can be taught only by segregating pupils and turning them over at special hours to separate representatives of rival faiths? This would be deliberately to adopt a scheme which is predicated upon the maintenance of social divisions in just the matter, religion, which is empty and futile save as it expresses the basic unities of life. An acute English critic has recently called us, with much truth, a "nation of villagers." But in this matter of education at least we have no intention or desire of letting go our hard-won state-consciousness in order to relapse into divisive provinciality. We are far, indeed, from having attained an explicit and articulated consciousness of the religious significance of democracy in education, and of education in democracy. But some underlying convictions get ingrained in the unconscious habit and find expression in obscure intimation and intense labor, long before they receive consistent theoretic formulation. In such a dim, blind, but effective way the American people is conscious

> We certainly cannot teach religion as an abstract essence. We have got to teach *something* as religion, and that means practically *some* religion.
>
> P. 80

These excerpts come from "Religion and Our Schools," an essay originally published in *The Hibbert Journal*, July, 1908. They are reprinted here from *Education Today*, 1940.

John Dewey argues that "scientific" education has made the notion of the supernatural "incredible," and anticipates "the coming of a fuller and deeper religion"—Humanism. Dewey viewed public education as the vehicle to promote this "deeper religion."

> **[T]he American people is conscious that its schools serve best the cause of religion in serving the cause of social unification. . . .**

that its schools serve best the cause of religion in serving the cause of social unification; and that under certain conditions schools are more religious in substance and in promise without any of the conventional badges and machinery of religious instruction than they could be in cultivating these forms at the expense of a state-consciousness.

We may indeed question whether it is true that in any relative sense this is a peculiarly irreligious age. Absolutely speaking, it doubtless is so; but have superficiality, flippancy, and externality of life been such uniformly absent traits of past ages? Our historic imagination is at best slightly developed. We generalize and idealize the past egregiously. We set up little toys to stand as symbols for long centuries and the complicated lives of countless individuals. And we are still, even those who have nominally surrendered supernatural dogma, largely under the dominion of the ideas of those who have succeeded in identifying religion with the rites, symbols, and emotions associated with these dogmatic beliefs. As we see the latter disappearing, we think we are growing irreligious. For all we know, the integrity of mind which is loosening the hold of these things is potentially much more religious than all that it is displacing. It is increased knowledge of nature which has made supra-nature incredible, or at least difficult of belief. We measure the change from the standpoint of the supernatural and we call it irreligious. Possibly if we measured it from the standpoint of the natural piety it is fostering, the sense of the permanent and inevitable implication of nature and man in a common career and destiny, it would appear as the growth of religion. We take note of the decay of cohesion and influence among the religiously organized bodies of the familiar historic type, and again we conventionally judge religion to be on the decrease. But it may be that their decadence is the rise of a broader and more catholic principle of human intercourse and association which is too religious to tolerate these pretensions to monopolize truth and to make private possessions of spiritual insight and aspiration.

It may be so; it may be that the symptoms of religious ebb as conventionally interpreted are symptoms of the coming of a fuller and deeper religion. I do not claim to know. But of one thing I am quite sure: our ordinary opinions about the rise and falling off of religion are highly conventional, based mostly upon the acceptance of a standard of religion which is the product of just those things in historic religions which are ceasing to be credible. So far as education is concerned, those who believe in religion as a natural expression of human experience must devote themselves to the development of the ideas of life which lie implicit in our still new science and our still newer democracy. They must interest themselves in the transformation of those institutions which still bear the dogmatic and the feudal stamp (and which do not?) till they are in accord with these ideas. In performing this service, it is their business to do what they can to prevent all public educational agencies from being employed in ways which inevitably impede the recognition of the spiritual import of science and of democracy, and hence of that type of religion which will be the fine flower of the modern spirit's achievement.

> **[I]t is their business to do what they can to prevent all public educational agencies from being employed in ways which inevitably impede the recognition of the spiritual import of science and of democracy, and hence of that type of religion which will be the fine flower of the modern spirit's achievement.**

Exhibit 3

1918

THE
NEXT STEP IN RELIGION

AN ESSAY TOWARD THE
COMING RENAISSANCE

BY
ROY WOOD SELLARS, Ph.D.
Author of "Critical Realism," "The Next
Step in Democracy," etc.

New York
THE MACMILLAN COMPANY
1918

"The center of gravity of religion has been openly changing for some time now from supernaturalism to what may best be called a humanistic naturalism . . . . There have been many steps forward in the past, for every age must possess its own religion, a religion concordant with its knowledge and expressive of its problems and aims."

FROM THE FOREWORD

"The coming phase of religion will reflect man's power over nature and his moral courage in the face of the facts and possibilities of life. It will be a religion of action and passion, a social religion, a religion of goals and prospects. It will be a free man's religion, a religion for an adult and aspiring democracy."

FROM THE FOREWORD

Roy Wood Sellars, a former president of the New York chapter of the American Humanist Association, and author of the *Humanist Manifesto I* (1933), makes the case for atheistic, naturalistic Humanism as the next world religion.

"But the humanist's religion is the religion of one who says yea to life here and now, of one who is self-reliant and fearless, intelligent and creative. It is the religion of the will to power, of one who is hard on himself and yet joyous in himself. It is the religion of courage and purpose and transforming energy. Its motto is, 'What hath not man wrought?' Its goal is the mastery of all things that they may become servants and instrumentalities to man's spiritual comradeship. Whatever mixture of magic, fear, ritual and adoration religion may have been in man's early days, it is now, and henceforth must be, that which concerns man's nobilities, his discovery of, and loyalty to, the pervasive values of life. The religious man will now be he who seeks out causes to be loyal to, social mistakes to correct, wounds to heal, achievements to further. He will be constructive, fearless, loyal, sensitive to the good wherever found, a believer in mankind, a fighter for things worth while."   p. 212

"The religion of human possiblities needs prophets who will grip men's souls with their description of a society in which righteousness, wisdom and beauty will reign together. . . . Loyalty to such an ideal will surely constitute the heart of the humanist's religion."   pp. 215-216

"If religion is to survive, it must be human and social. It is they who insist upon a supernatural foundation and object who are its enemies. Man's life is spiritual in its own right. So long as he shall dream of beauty and goodness and truth his life will not lack religion."   p. 225

Exhibit 4

1922

EDUCATION TODAY

By JOHN DEWEY

Edited and with a Foreword by
JOSEPH RATNER

What the best and wisest parent wants for his own child, that must the community want for all its children. Any other ideal for our schools is narrow and unlovely; acted upon it destroys our democracy.—JOHN DEWEY

G . P . PUTNAM'S SONS . *New York*

We make a religion of our education, we profess unbounded faith in its possibilities, we point with pride to its advance, we term instruction an art and school management a profession. Faith in education signifies nothing less than belief in the possibility of deliberate direction of the formation of human disposition and intelligence. P. 145

If we have any ground to be religious about anything, we may take education religiously. P. 147

Note: These excerpts come from "Education as Religion," an article written by Dewey which originally appeared in *The New Republic*, September 13, 1922. It was reprinted in *Education Today*, a 1940 publication.

John Dewey, a signatory of the *Humanist Manifesto I*, clearly identifies education as a religious experience. The religion he believed should be imparted to the next generation, of course, denied all hints of the supernatural.

Exhibit 5

1926

HUMANISM

by

CURTIS W. REESE

THE OPEN COURT PUBLISHING COMPANY
CHICAGO   1926   LONDON

"HUMANIZING RELIGION"

CONTENTS

Charles Francis Potter described Curtis W. Reese as one of the two or three founders of modern Humanism. Reese believed this new religion should be applied to every facet of reality. Reese signed *Humanist Manifesto I*.

> **Religion symbolizes the human quest to discover in the nature of man and the universe the kind of life that is inherently desirable. . . . This quest is man's religion.**

PART III

HUMANIZING RELIGION (continued)

A WORD is a symbol of reality. This is true whether the reality be a perceptual fact or conceptual theory. When reality changes, clear thinking requires that the old symbol be exchanged for another or that the change in content be clearly recorded. When a word symbolizes a movement with continuity of problem and of attempt at solution, the familiar symbol should be kept and its changed meaning recorded. Psychology is a case in point. Once psychology was a name of the science that dealt with the *soul*; later of the science that dealt with *mental faculties*; then of the science that dealt with *states* of *consciousness*; and now psychology is the name of the science that deals with *behavior*. The old symbol still holds. Much more should this be true when the symbol is weighted with sacred associations and memories. Religion is a symbol which not only has continuity of problem and of attempt at solution but which is also surrounded with the most hallowed associations and memories. Religion symbolizes the human quest to discover in the nature of man and the universe the kind of life that is inherently desirable, and to enlist in its behalf all instrumentalities, both human and cosmic, that

22   HUMANISM

are capable of assisting in its realization. This quest is man's religion. In early religions the quest took the form of attempts on the part of man to relate himself to those instrumentalities and values that seemed to have significance for the welfare of the group; and later it took the form of attempts to placate the personal gods in order to gain personal peace. While the forms of religion have undergone revolution, we shall retain the term "religion." My chief purpose, however, is not to justify the word but to record certain changes in its content and form.

The common denominator of the old religions is found in *man's response to super-human sources of fortune*. This belief in and relation to super-human sources of fortune is characteristic of the old religions. Without this psychological situation the old faiths cannot admit the religious validity of any human behavior. Hence the old religions have resulted in a servile psychological attitude.

This pathetic and tragic outcome of the old religions is now somewhat relieved by humanistic tendencies which are gradually growing everywhere. Modern thinkers are finding the content of religion in human worths and its cosmic significance in man's co-operation with and control of the processes of life to the end that human possibilities shall be completely and harmoniously realized. Humanism aims at the conscious experience of the fullness of life. It regards this as the aim and end of religion and

> **While the forms of religion have undergone revolution, we shall retain the term "religion."**

of all social instrumentalities. In other words, humanism stands for the complete and permanent satisfactions of human life.

The object of the old religion is the superhuman unknown and the chief content of the old religion is the sentiment entertained toward the superhuman unknown. The object of humanism is *life*, and its chief content is *loyalty* to life. In the old religion right and wrong are defined in terms of conformity to standards extrinsic to human life; in humanism right and wrong are defined in terms of consequence to human life. The old religion is characterized by trust and receptivity; humanism, by aspiration and creativity.

Whatever theological significance is inferred from or attached to humanism, it is functional, tenative, secondary. The old religion judges man by his contribution to the gods; humanism judges the gods by their contribution to man. In the old religion theological beliefs are central and imperative; in humanism theological theories are types of "spiritual short hand." In the old religion a theological revolution is spiritual treason; in humanism a theological revolution is a change of mental attitude, a shifting of postulates, a minor part of the day's work.

According to the old view, religion without superhuman objects of faith is impossible. But if religion is the quest of man to discover and live the inherently desirable life, manifestly theological convic-

[I]n humanism right and wrong are defined in terms of consequence to human life.

[H]umanistic religion does not regard the acceptance of any philosophical theory or theological hypothesis as religiously necessary.

tions and philosophies of the ultimate nature of the universe are not prerequisite to the religious life. Religion is not constituted of theology or philosophy or metaphysics—but it may use them as instruments in the enhancement of human life. Man may be utterly void of theology and yet be deeply religious. Religion is enhanced by various intellectual and aesthetic devices, such as philosophical theories and liturgical forms, but none of them is exclusively essential.

In the theocentric world of the pre-scientific days man wanted super powers or beings whom he could placate and so secure special agency. But science has discredited special agency. It has found the universe to be a self-operating system. It finds ordinary cosmic events and processes routine and impersonal, and other things cared for by highly specialized parts of nature such as man. It regards order and purpose as self existent. Reality is found, but its ultimate nature is not yet determined. Man's whole world outlook is vastly different from what it once was and it is still subject to change. Hence humanistic religion does not regard the acceptance of any philosophical or theological hypothesis as religiously necessary.

Yet, in order to make its committals effective in the realization of its goals, humanism needs a science of values. Such a science must be evolved through long experimentation. It must be founded on enlightened experience, true to basic desires, and

Exhibit 6

1927

Humanist Sermons

Edited by
CURTIS W. REESE

Sermons by

JOHN HAYNES HOLMES
CHARLES H. LYTTLE
CURTIS W. REESE
E. STANTON HODGIN
E. BURDETTE BACKUS
A. WAKEFIELD SLATEN
JOHN H. DIETRICH
EARL F. COOK
EUGENE MILNE COSGROVE
L. M. BIRKHEAD
E. CALDECOTT
SIDNEY S. ROBINS
FREDERICK M. ELIOT
JAMES H. HART
FRANK S. C. WICKS
FRANK C. DOAN
AUTHUR L. WEATHERLY
A. EUSTACE HAYDON

CHICAGO : LONDON
The Open Court Publishing Company
1927

"Within the liberal churches of America there is a religious movement which has come to be known as Humanism."

Preface

Within the liberal churches of America there is a religious movement which has come to be known as Humanism. The ideology of this movement I attempted to sketch in "Humanism," issued last year. The present volume is a collection of sermons which have been used in the regular course of parish preaching. Each minister was asked to make his own selection. Consequently, the wide range and supplementary character of the subjects are purely accidental.

It is not my function to analyze or evaluate the sermons. Each minister has spoken his own mind in his own way, and is alone responsible for his utterance.

My aim is to introduce the Humanist point of view in a way that will assist the proper interpretation of the sermons that follow.

Humanism has been used to designate certain thought movements which in varying degrees have centered attention on the study, the worth, and the enhancement of human life.

Sophist Humanism, in the fifth century B.C., turned attention from cosmological speculation to the study of man. Renaissance Humanism, beginning in the fourteenth century, flooded the dark ages with the light of classical learning, thus assisting mightily in transforming the medieval into the modern world. Encyclopedic Humanism, in the second half of the eighteenth century, fought error, fostered enlightenment, and magnified human desires and aspirations. In current history,

v

Curtis W. Reese, a signatory of *Humanist Manifesto I*, edited *Humanist Sermons*. These essays are self-described "sermons" because they were delivered from the pulpit in various liberal/Humanist churches.

> **There is a large element of faith in all religion. [Christianity has faith] in the love of God; and Humanism in man as the measure of values.**

The Faith of Humanism
Curtis W. Reese

THERE is a large element of faith in all religion. Buddhism has faith in the inexorable laws of Karma; Mohammedanism in the unyielding will of Allah; Confucianism in the moral nature of Heaven; Christianity in the love of God; and Humanism in man as the measure of values.

There is a large element of faith in all philosophy. Idealists have faith in eternal values; Realists in the objective reality of facts; Naturalists in an inner survival urge; and Pragmatists in the workableness of truth.

There is a large measure of faith in all science. Faith in the orderliness of nature and in man's mind to comprehend it makes science possible. There could be no science if we began with chaos on the part of the universe and incompetency on the part of man.

There is a large element of faith in all human relations. The foundations of government, the warp and woof of economic relations, and especially the very structure of the home, partake in large measure of the nature of faith.

Hypotheses, postulates, and assumptions in their proper realm are comparable to faith in the realm of religion. In this way I speak of the faith of Humanism.

39

---

40   *Humanist Sermons*

Competent philosophers, scientists, and even theologians, regard working assumptions as tentative. They constantly check for error; they diligently gather new data and re-examine the old generalizations in the light of the new facts. They welcome criticism and verification from competent persons. Their faith is consciously experimental. And it is thus with the faith of the Humanist.

Humanism aims to comprehend man in his total setting; to know him as a child of the cosmos, as the individual member of the human group, and as the parent of civilizations yet to be. It sets as its definite goal, not knowledge for its own sake but knowledge as a means to the enrichment of human life. Here it attacks its problems with evangelical fervor and summons to its cause all knowledge, all faith, all hope, and all love.

Let us sketch the faith of Humanism in broad outline and see what it has to offer.

I

In the first place, Humanism has faith in the trustworthiness of the scientific spirit and method; viz., freedom of inquiry and controlled experiment. Fundamentalism is skeptical of science; Modernism merely flirts with science; but Humanism says that, while science may give us inadequate knowledge, it gives all we have and we must make the most of it. Upon science and the legitimate inferences from its established facts we are dependent for our knowledge of the nature of the universe, of the evolution of life, and of man's prowess and possibilities. And how stimulating yet sobering it is to contemplate the universe of modern science!

(1) With the destruction of old cosmologies went many a man's sense of being at home in the uni-

> **Hypotheses, postulates, and assumptions in their proper realm are comparable to faith in the realm of religion. In this way I speak of the faith of Humanism.**

Exhibit 7

1927

Humanist Sermons

Edited by
CURTIS W. REESE

Sermons by

JOHN HAYNES HOLMES
CHARLES H. LYTTLE
CURTIS W. REESE
E. STANTON HODGIN
E. BURDETTE BACKUS
A. WAKEFIELD SLATEN
JOHN H. DIETRICH
EARL F. COOK
EUGENE MILNE COSGROVE
L. M. BIRKHEAD
E. CALDECOTT
SIDNEY S. ROBINS
FREDERICK M. ELIOT
JAMES H. HART
FRANK S. C. WICKS
FRANK C. DOAN
AUTHUR L. WEATHERLY
A. EUSTACE HAYDON

CHICAGO : LONDON
The Open Court Publishing Company
1927

> ❝This nation . . .
> committed its life
> to the humanistic
> position long before
> such a faith was
> thought of as a
> religion.❞

60   *Humanist Sermons*

supreme importance, while human wisdom was thought of as being not only of secondary moment but as often obscuring and hindering divine revelation.

Our nation followed a diametrically opposite course. It disestablished the church, letting theology shift for itself. It in no sense repudiated religion, only declaring it to be an individual matter and no concern of the state. In place of the church that it had disestablished, it established the school, giving it state aid and authority, thus making education, human wisdom, knowledge of the world forces that impinge upon us the bulwark of national security and stability. This nation thus committed its life to the humanistic position long before such a faith was thought of as a religion. As a matter of fact, religion in its most nascent form is seldom ever recognized as religion at all. Not until it has lost some of its incipient power and has crystallized into a self-conscious theological system is it institutionalized and given sanctity. Humanism is still too vitally diffused, too undifferentiated from life to be admitted into the pantheon.

All Americans are humanists. They find guidance in the accumulations of knowledge and experience that mankind has gathered from its contacts with the world forces and its adjustments to them. Chief reliance is upon the educational and cultural forces that give enlightenment.

A vast majority of Americans are also theists. In addition to the general body of worldly knowledge and experience upon which they freely draw for guidance, they feel that they have access also to a personal divinity from whom they may receive additional guidance of a higher and more sacred character.

Many hold their theistic faith more or less tentatively and confusedly. They assent to it for traditional

One of the Humanist "sermons" that impressed Curtis W. Reese was written by E. Stanton Hodgin. Hodgin asserts that the public schools took the place of the church in America, and that the schools are based on the religion of Humanism.

> 66 Humanism thus
> seems to be gaining
> almost everything
> except recognition as
> a religious faith. 99

E. Stanton Hodgin 61

and associational reasons. They feel that they have here something in reserve that cushions them to a certain extent against the hard realities of life, but it seldom affects their serious decisions in the important affairs of life.

Others hold to it with fanatical zeal and so far as in their power lies would compel everyone to bend the knee to it. They would reverse the position of the founders of our nation, would make this nation theistic in name at least, and would put all education in leading strings to theology as it was in the centuries of the past.

To many of even the more fanatical theists, their theological faith is exotic. They bow down to it, render it obeisance and would compel others to do the same, would fight for it and willingly die for it, if need be; but, having done it outward reverence, they turn from it and guide their lives almost wholly by the same general body of worldly knowledge we all draw upon, freely using and enjoying the fruits of the sciences they condemn.

Even the churches—born of the intense theism of the Middle Ages and still maintaining the extreme theistic expressions and forms in their services of worship—are becoming more and more humanistic in character. Catholic and fundamentalist churches no less than modernists are becoming increasingly centers of worldly culture and discipline upon which the people depend for guidance in their daily lives rather than upon their theology.

Humanism thus seems to be gaining almost everything except recognition as a religious faith. Since the fact remains that humanism is the dominant force in our modern life, institutional recognition is a matter of minor importance.

Exhibit 8

1928

RELIGION COMING OF AGE

BY

ROY WOOD SELLARS, Ph.D.

PROFESSOR OF PHILOSOPHY, UNIVERSITY OF MICHIGAN,
AUTHOR OF "EVOLUTIONARY NATURALISM,"
"THE NEXT STEP IN RELIGION," ETC.

New York
THE MACMILLAN COMPANY
1928

"The present book is an attempt to show the import of this recent development for religion. Its keynote is the union of humanism and naturalism. The spiritual must be naturalized and humanized; but it is equally true that the scientific view of the world requires deepening and illumination. . . . Moreover, human and social evolution must be taken seriously and fitted into the scheme of things. It is this result that the new naturalism is making possible. Something of this wider and more humanistic perspective I have tried to put into this book. A religion founded on realities is a religion coming of age."

[vi]

Roy Wood Sellars, author of *Humanist Manifesto I*, claims that traditional religion is dying and Humanism is the coming new religion. In 1955, Sellars was honored as a "Humanist Pioneer" by the American Humanist Association.

> "There are two directions which liberalism is taking; the one we may call *mysticism*, the other we may call *humanism*."

RELIGION COMING OF AGE

Modernism and Fundamentalism in Protestantism

Each Protestant church has its own variety of internal struggle, and it would obviously be impossible to go into detail. I shall take the situation in America as typical.

Fundamentalism represents an aggressive attack by those who accept the traditional beliefs against what they feel to be the insidious encroachment of science and liberal thought. It is not led by great theologians familiar with church history but rather by preachers trained in the ways of political democracy. I do not wish to do injustice to their pronouncements, for they are evidently sincere, but they do strike the philosopher as expressions of an outlook tinged with Mediaevalism. With this qualification, it is undeniable that the fundamentalists stand for what we may call popular dogmatic Christianity. The riddle they are propounding is this, When does Christianity cease to be Christianity? Our fathers believed in the virgin birth; do we? Our fathers believed in miracles; so we? Our fathers believed in Christ's atonement for sin; do we? If we don't, we are not Christians.

Well, it was not a bad thing to have the issue raised. What was unlovely was the spirit of persecution and intolerance that went with the movement. That smacked at times of a union of Church and State.

The following quotation from a book by E. U. Mullins called *Christianity at the Crossroads* illustrates the fundamentalist position very well: "The issues as to fact concern the person of Jesus Christ. All other issues turn upon this 'What think ye of Christ? Was he supernatural in origin? Was he sinless in character? Did he perform miracles? Was his death on the cross an atonement for sin? Did his crucified body come forth from the grave in resurrection

[124]

THE PRESENT SITUATION

power?' These are the crucial questions. . . . To deny the facts themselves is to evolutionize Christianity."

What we may call liberalism is usually less sure of itself and its beliefs. That is but natural in an age of transition. One of the best characterizations of liberalism is that of Dr. Parks, who calls it "a state of mind." This state of mind consists of openness to the streams of culture of the present.

There are two directions which liberalism is taking; the one we may call *mysticism*, the other we may call *humanism*. And, of course, these tendencies may be blended in various degrees. From a recent volume of sermons called *Humanist Sermons*, edited by Curtis Reese, I select a passage or so as typical of what seems to me the humanist direction. "To me," writes E. Burdette Backus, "the signs are clear that humanity has struck its tents and is again on the march towards a new religious faith which I dare to believe will provide us with a religion greater than Christianity, greater than any of the historic faiths of the past, though I am keenly aware that that which I call religion will seem to many earnest men and women not religion at all, but rather irreligion.... The concern of the religion of the future will be human values, the enrichment of character, of personality, the creation of beauty, the discovery of truth."

Mysticism takes its departure from a peculiar kind of experience, largely of an emotional type. In it, there is often a belief in a communion with some spiritual being. It should be noted, however, that the ideas and interpretations which are associated with mysticism are always expressive of the cultural traditions. The Mohammedan or Hindu mystic does not sense this transcendent reality in the same way that the Roman Catholic or the Protestant mystic does.

[125]

> "[Humanity is] on the march towards a new religious faith which I dare to believe will provide us with a religion greater than Christianity. . . ."

A man's religion will be his imaginative realization of life.

My thesis is, that religion is something larger and more significant than what we have been told it was. Human life demands interpretation and vision if it is to secure unity, reasonableness, and passion; and is not such interpretation of the very essence of religion? If so, religion is as natural as human living itself. It is not something coming in from outside in a supernatural way. To some, it will be a philosophy of life; to others, a moral perspective; to still others, a code and loyalties. May we not say, then, that the very indefiniteness and conflict of objectives which we note around us to-day is a symptom of the inadequacy of religious traditions to the needs of the present? Is not the great lack of our times a religion adequate to our culture and its possiblities? We need, as never before, social and personal vision and a sense of human values. An inadequate religion has done us much harm.

To call traditional Christianity an inadequate religion will startle those who are dominated by mystical, and dramatic, personal loyalties. But we have seen that Christianity was *primarily* a salvation-religion with a supernatural perspective. This is not to deny the tremendous value and significance of an ethical attitude which it contained. The portrait of Jesus has been its ethical strength. Historically, true in detail or not, it yet presented under high sanctions, to the imagination of the West, an ideal whose spirit was love and gentleness. And this note has been recurrent in the history of Christianity. In our humanitarian age it has sounded more and more loudly. But, when we look deeply into the situation, we realize that this element in Christianity is quite separable from the supernatural framework which it

[250]

"[R]eligion is something larger and more significant than what we have been told it was."

"The religion of humanism will be a growth due to, and resting on, the coöperative spiritual life to the making of which will go a multitude of minds and hearts."

An adequate religion must be full-blooded and alive to all domains of the spiritual life of man. It must yea-say human endeavour.

It follows that I am not arguing for a specific new religion with a revered founder, analogous to those of the past and represented in this country by Christian Science and Mormonism. The day of that kind of religion is, I hope, waning. It is assuredly past for educated people in touch with science and philosophy. The religion of humanism will be a growth due to, and resting on, the coöperative spiritual life to the making of which will go a multitude of minds and hearts. And, once we have secured true historical perspective, we may well speak of it as a new reformation of Christianity, but a reformation far deeper and more significant than that of the sixteenth century. In a very real sense, each generation has its own religion. There is continuity, but there is also novelty. Let us, therefore, take Christianity, not as something revealed once for all to the Fathers, but as a term for our Western spiritual life. Once we have cut the supposed bonds with a supernatural world, we see that religion is, and has always been, a social product. What would Jesus have been without the insights which he inherited from his Jewish past and which he absorbed in the synagogue? I do not for a moment wish to belittle the rôle of the great man in society, but we must always see him in his social setting. The texture of his life is social and its setting is social. What he can add is a creative ferment and the suggestions of new combinations.

To the humanist, then, with his social naturalism, man's spiritual life is like a mighty stream to which there are many tributaries. It is said that Erasmus put Socrates in the calendar of his saints. *Sancta Socrate, ora pro nobis.* The

[252]

1928

66 Now I am convinced that the humanistic religion into which Christianity will gradually be transformed will correct this mistake. 99

CHAPTER XVI

RELIGION COMING OF AGE

In this final chapter I wish to summarize my conclusion, draw certain implications and make a few suggestions.

The spiritual life of man, we have argued, is a growth and has passed through stages which are more or less distinct. It began in a cry of supplication to the mysterious powers of life and death; it was caught up into the magnetic influence of the belief in another world and thereby became a religion of salvation, yearning for Heaven and fearful of Hell; finally, it is in our own day clearly shifting to a religion of this life with its problems and possibilities. Religion and humanity have been organic to one another. The progress of one has been bound up with the growth of the other. In a rough way, we may speak of these stages of religion as corresponding to the childhood of the race, its romantic adolescence, and its maturity. Religion is coming of age.

In all these stages, the dynamics of religion has lain in what man valued and believed. Long ago man could peer but a short way into himself and his world and he felt himself helpless before the powers which surrounded him. And so he danced before his gods and gave them burnt offerings. But, with the growth of culture and self-consciousness, man came to think of himself as a soul imprisoned in a body. Nature became the scene of a tremendous drama in which gods fought with demons for man's soul. Prophets arose who told him that there was a way of sal-

[275]

"Because they are right." But I have a perfect right to ask how he knows that they are right, and what he means by right. In other words, reflection is bound to raise questions which are not natural to custom. The moral categories of right and wrong, good and bad, conscience and duty, need analysis. Now it is unfortunate that the Christian tradition was not intrinsically philosophic to this extent. Its morality has been one of inspiration rather than one of reflection. I would be the last one to deny the value of inspiration in morality but this approach can be overdone. One of the weaknesses of the religious tradition lies in its mystical attitude towards morality. Since this was combined with an ingredient of theological hedonism, it gave a wrong slant to the popular thought of morality. It made morality something supernatural and more or less irrational.

Now I am convinced that the humanistic religion into which Christianity will gradually be transformed will correct this mistake. Moral philosophy can be of great assistance here. In what follows I shall try to indicate the principles which seem to me correct. Obviously, I cannot develop them in detail, but the interested reader will find a similar outlook in a companion volume of this series by Professor Drake, entitled *The New Morality*, a book devoted entirely to ethical questions. May I say again how important I think this reflective approach to morality is? It is very unfortunate that, in this country at least, to say that a question, like prohibition, has become a religious issue means that people take an emotional, and almost fanatical, attitude towards it. Our evangelical tradition needs cross-fertilization with philosophy.

The ethical position which is slowly arising in philosophy may be described as experimental humanism. Much reflec-

[270]

66 In a rough way, we may speak of these stages of religion as corresponding to the childhood of the race, its romantic adolescence, and its maturity. Religion is coming of age. 99

Exhibit 9

1930

CHARLES FRANCIS POTTER

HVMANISM
A NEW RELIGION

MCMXXX
SIMON AND SCHUSTER
NEW YORK
[1930]

"[Humanism] is a new type of religion altogether."

THE ADVENT OF HUMANISM IN RELIGION

the real values of the ideas, "God," "prayer," and "worship," may be retained, the present concepts, and perhaps even the words themselves, must sooner or later be abandoned.

So Humanism is not simply another denomination of Protestant Christianity; it is not a creed; not is it a cult.

It is a new type of religion altogether.

It is a new way of looking at religion. You have to make over and broaden your definition of religion to get Humanism in at all, especially if you come from a Christian background. The Humanist splits the seams of all the old coats of religion when he tries them on. The new wine has burst the old wine-skins.

The coming of Humanism is so great a change in religion that its significance will be apparent only as people become aware of its implications, probably a generation hence.

Apparently there has been a suddenness in the advent of Humanism. A few months ago one heard of it only in a very limited circle: today the word is on everybody's lips. Newspapers and magazines one picks up are full of it. Religious weeklies have little else in them these days save discussions of Humanism.

But the suddenness is only apparent. Humanism has been quietly growing in the minds of a few, waiting until the spread of scientific knowledge should prepare the way for its appearing. Persons familiar with trends in religious thought have for some time sensed a mighty change impending.

The revolution in religion they foresaw is here.

By revolution in religion we do not mean mere

3

Although a Baptist minister for more than a decade, Charles Francis Potter left the church to work as a Unitarian minister. After another decade, Potter opted to describe himself as a "Humanist minister." He is a signatory of *Humanist Manifesto I.*

> ❝ Is Humanism
> a religion?
> It is both a
> religion and
> a philosophy
> of culture. ❞

HUMANISM: A NEW RELIGION

But Mr. Lippmann and Mr. Krutch are rejected as Humanists by the main body of academic Humanists in the symposium edited by Norman Foerster, entitled *Humanism and America*, including contributions by Irving Babbitt, Paul Elmer More, and T. S. Eliot. It seems that Messrs. Lippmann and Krutch are too revolutionary and that "The New Humanism is Revolt against Revolt—the keynote of culture for the 1930's."

The Foerster, More, Babbitt group of academic Humanists opposes with vehemence both the extreme naturalism of Krutch and also the belief in man and the revolt against supernaturalism which characterizes the religious Humanists.

The academic Humanists deserve applause for their defense of the dignity and integrity of the individual in this day of success-worship and standardization. With them on that issue the religious Humanists gladly stand. But academic Humanism of the type represented in this symposium is alarmist in temper, orthodox in tendency and likely to degenerate into a new scholasticism. Much that is human is alien to it.

Is Humanism a religion? It is both a religion and a philosophy of culture. Academic or classical Humanists and religious Humanists both have a right to the name, but if they wish to avoid misunderstandings, they will both do well to prefix a qualifying adjective to the word Humanism.

114

HUMANISM: A NEW RELIGION

Education is thus a most powerful ally of Humanism, and every American public school is a school of Humanism. What can the theistic Sunday-schools, meeting for an hour once a week, and teaching only a fraction of the children, do to stem the tide of a five-day program of humanistic teaching?

The Pope and the Fundamentalists see the danger to Theism. The former would have all Catholic parents send their children to parochial schools where they can be given theistic antidotes to counteract the humanist poison so prevalent in American life! The Fundamentalists concentrate their opposition on the theory of evolution, sensing that there lies a great danger to theistic religion.

So very humanistic is modern education that no religion has a future unless it be Humanism. The religion of tomorrow in America and of the day after tomorrow in all the world may not be in all respects identical with the religious Humanism we are advocating in this book, but it will be mightily like it and of the same spirit.

One American educator, Dr. John Dewey, from whom the new type of modern education received its impetus and much of its method, and who is also best acquainted with the progress of education round the world, has this to say (*Forum*, March 1930) of great interest to all who are studying religious Humanism and the future of religion:

"I would suggest that the future religion is connected with the possibility of developing a faith in the possibilities of human experience and human relationships that will create a vital sense

128

> ❝ Education
> is the most
> powerful ally
> of Humanism,
> and every
> American
> public school
> is a school
> of Humanism. ❞

HUMANIST RELIGION

Exhibit 10

BY
CURTIS W. REESE
*Author of "Humanism," editor of
"Humanist Sermons"*

NEW YORK
THE MACMILLAN COMPANY
1931

> **"** . . . Humanism is making itself felt in religious circles. **"**

INTRODUCTION

It may be that there would be some advantage in starting a movement *de novo*, provided of course one could find a basic idea that had no history. However this may be, Humanism has a history and must make the most of it. The Humanist idea has found expression in varying forms in many lands and among many peoples. Any idea that is vital grows through the years. It is not to be expected that such an idea will always be consistent in details. It is enough if there is continuity of fundamental purpose.

Valid Humanist movements, however they may differ in minor respects, have this in common, viz., (1) the centering of attention upon human interests, (2) the use, the control, and the altering of reality for human ends, and (3) the holding of doctrines as hypothetical and ideals as tentative.

To-day, as never before, Humanism is making itself felt in religious circles. Throughout the world good and able persons are alarmed over its spread. Sincere and earnest ministers misrepresent and denounce it. Certain religious journals flay it without mercy. Pious persons who are otherwise tolerant quiver with fear and rage at the mention of it.

I myself have no interest in Humanism merely as a
5

INTRODUCTION
6
doctrine of protest, nor as a type of criticism, and much less as an anti-ecclesiastical complex. My concern is for humanism as a philosophy of life—in sharp contrast with opposing schools of thought—able to challenge the traditional philosophies and ethnic religions, having a program covering all aspects of human well-being, and aiming at the complete possession of the territory of the human spirit. Short of this, Humanism would merely add another to the already overcrowded field of warring sects.

Rigorous thinking on a factual basis is one of the greatest needs of to-day. The temptation to slovenly thought is great, but religious leaders cannot afford to succumb to it, nor can they successfully dodge philosophical issues by avowing practical aims. The philosophical and the practical are forever intertwined; that is, theory and practice go together. The chapters that follow are experiments in this direction.

A Unitarian minister who firmly believed that Humanism should aim for "complete possession of the territory of the human spirit," Curtis W. Reese is rightly regarded as one of the leaders of twentieth century Humanism.

41

> **" [T]he trend is away from . . . the notion that religion is necessarily tied up with any theistic interpretation of cosmic existence."**

52   HUMANIST RELIGION

and beauty? What of minds freed of the fears that haunt them—fear of the past that presses upon them, fear of the overarching unknown, fear of the plagues that waste the body and the mind, fear of fear itself? These are causes that will give dramatic content to effective preaching in a humanized world.

The trend is away from doctrines considered as authoritative pronouncements about the eternal, and in the direction of doctrine considered as the orderly arrangement of convictions about everyday life.

RELIGION

(1) Thus may be seen the necessity for a re-statement of the nature of religion itself. Here again the trend is away from religion understood as man's response to "the determiner of destiny," to use Professor Pratt's terms, or even as man's response to superhuman sources of fortune; away from religion understood as "man's conduct facing Godward," as I was taught in my theological school days; away from the fascinating and poetic theory that religion is "the life of God in the soul of man"; away also from the notion that religion is necessarily tied up with any theistic interpretation of cosmic existence.

Rather is the trend in the way of regarding religion as a human effort to find satisfactory modes of living, in the course of which many personal, social, planetary, and cosmological theories may be postulated, tested, and abandoned; the abiding thing being the urge to newer and newer efforts to reach ever receding goals.

MODERN RELIGIOUS DEVELOPMENTS   53

It is the testimony of Professor A. Eustace Haydon, of the Department of Comparative Religion in the University of Chicago, that to-day in practically all religions there are increasing numbers who interpret religion as the shared quest for a satisfying life.

(2) The very vernacular use of the term *religion* is tending to hasten the identification of religion with the questing process. When a man commits himself to a great *cause* we say that cause becomes his religion. We speak of men who make their art or their business or their social theory, their religion. Communism is said to be the religion of young Russia, as indeed it is.

Not long ago I attended an experience meeting in an orthodox Christian church where some ten or a dozen men testified. Every man of them told of his religion experience in terms of ceasing to do this and beginning to do that. Unconsciously they revealed the real nature of their religion. It was a human doing and not doing. The only trouble was that they were concerned with doing and not doing inconsequential things, such as card playing. But they identified religious experience with human behavior in a human setting.

A few years ago I had occasion to argue a matter before a commission studying a certain problem relating to theological education, of which commission the late Charles W. Eliot was a member. In the course of the discussion one of the commission, himself an overseer of Harvard, remarked that he was not interested in a type of theological education that turned out what

> **" When a man commits himself to a great *cause* we say that cause becomes his religion."**

he called "social secretaries." Whereupon, Dr. Eliot, in his characteristically direct way said, "My dear sir, if I am not badly mistaken, within the next twenty-five or thirty years our idea of the very nature of religion will undergo a great change." That change is taking place even more rapidly than President Eliot predicted. To-day great religious organizations are committing themselves to concrete quests. One of the most effective examples of this is the work of the Federal Council of the Churches of Christ in America. Practically all the great religious movements, including Catholic, Protestant, and Jewish, have within the last ten years issued far reaching programs of social reconstruction.

(3) It is not likely that religion will cease to concern itself with the effort to understand man's cosmic setting, nor should it abandon such effort. It is natural that man should forever attempt to push back the veil of mystery that hangs so tantalizingly about him. Modern minds are well aware how painfully inadequate is our total knowledge; but they feel that the little knowledge man does possess is his instrument and his hope of further conquests of the dark. In controlling life situations a little factual knowledge is worth worlds of mystery.

Religion as thus understood is developing new ideals and techniques for accomplishing its purpose. Fact finding becomes more significant than wishful petition. What man really wants becomes of more concern than what it has been said that he should want. Æsthetic

❝Religion as thus understood is developing new ideals and techniques for accomplishing its purpose.❞

❝In summary, the trend in modern religious developments is away from the transcendent, the authoritative, the dogmatic, and toward the human, the experimental, the tentative . . .❞

expression is regarded as superior to monastic repression. Scientific apparatus ranks higher than sacred images. The free play of free minds replaces the submissive will. The buoyant thrill of physical and mental well-being are of first importance in spiritual well-being. Modern religion says to mankind, trust your capacity to understand increasingly the universe in which you live; trust your ability to order your way increasingly in harmony with the possibilities that inhere in the nature of man and the world; and so trusting, act accordingly.

In summary, the trend in modern religious developments is away from the transcendent, the authoritative, the dogmatic, and toward the human, the experimental, the tentative; away from the abnormal, the formal, the ritualistic; and toward the normal, the informal, the usual; away from the extraordinary mystic expression, the exalted mood, the otherworldly; and toward the ethical, the social and the worldly; away from religion conceived as one man's concerns, and toward religion conceived as man's one concern.

Exhibit 11

1933

Humanism

By

JOHN H. DIETRICH, D.D.

*Minister of the First Unitarian Society,
Minneapolis, Minn., since 1916.*

*Prepared at the request of the American
Unitarian Association,
December, 1933.*

[No. 337]

AMERICAN UNITARIAN ASSOCIATION
25 Beacon Street, Boston, Mass.

66 [Religion] must also
become naturalistic
and humanistic. 99

Humanism 11

lous situation of a genuine scientific and social progress on the one hand, and on the other an ossified religion, seeking to conserve an ancient philosophy and polity. Two ideas are here in conflict—on the one hand, man organizing and directing his own life, on the other, professing to believe that a deity orders it for him. Between the two there can be no reconciliation, and religion will eventually have to give way to the facts. Which means that religion, if it would be a vital factor in human life, must also become naturalistic and humanistic. That it is seeking to do so is evidenced on every hand. It is the growing tendency of the part of Modernists to place a naturalistic and humanistic interpretation upon religion that causes so much disturbance within the Protestant denominations; while there has grown up within the liberal churches of America a very definite movement known as Humanism, which is seeking to ground religion in human living rather than in some supernatural existence, by interpreting the good life in terms of human values and by directing man's religious aspirations toward the enhancement of human life.

II

I want to emphasize the tremendous revolution of thought which this entails, and which accounts for the confusion and the reservations, the compromises and the insincerities, of the present re-

66 [T]here has grown
up within the
liberal churches
of America a very
definite movement
known as
Humanism . . . 99

John H. Dietrich, a Unitarian minister and a signatory of *Humanist Manifesto I*, wrote this booklet to demonstrate that Humanism is the only viable religion for modern man.

> 66 Humanism thinks of religion as something very different and far deeper than any belief in God. To it, religion is . . . the upreaching and aspiring impulse in a human life. It is life striving for its completest fulfillment, and anything which contributes to this fulfillment is religious, whether it be associated with the idea of God or not. 99

ligion. For centuries, the idea of God has been the very heart of religion; it has been said "No God, no religion." But Humanism thinks of religion as something very different and far deeper than any belief in God. To it, religion is not the attempt to establish right relations with a supernatural being, but rather the upreaching and aspiring impulse in a human life. It is life striving for its completest fulfillment, and anything which contributes to this fulfillment is religious, whether it be associated with the idea of God or not.

This constitutes the greatest religious revolution the world has ever known. Many changes have come into the religious life of the past, but none so great as this. The world is so saturated with the theism and the supernaturalism of the Christian church that any other form of religious aspiration is regarded as impossible, if not unthinkable. Therefore, progress in this direction will, naturally, be slow. It took two centuries for the popular mind to become accustomed to the new ideas of the Copernican system in astronomy, and even now the ideas and phrases of Ptolemy still linger. Although thought moves faster today, it will take many years to work out the revolution in religious thought which Humanism involves, and even then we will probably find the old ideas and phrases of supernaturalism hanging on. We have many instances of this fact today. There are many ministers who are purely humanistic in their thinking and who call themselves Humanists, but who continue to use the theistic phraseology, and talk about God and prayer and

salvation, as if these words had a meaning in the new interpretation of life.

III

The logical implications of this naturalistic attitude toward the universe and this humanistic attitude toward human life leads to an entirely new type of religion, which perhaps is best described as naturalistic Humanism, and which involves a very definitely changed attitude and a very definite world-view.

First, a few words in regard to the changed attitude. Having adopted the scientific point of view, the Humanist dismisses every suggestion of the supernatural and advocates giving our entire attention to the problems of man and his adjustment to his physical environment and his social surroundings. Until recently the great religions of mankind were devoted to the attempt to know and exploit the supernatural, which our primitive ancestors constructed out of the "vivid but uninformed imaginations," while man's life on this planet was considered unimportant as compared to the immortal existence which was believed to await him after death. This earthly life was regarded only as a brief training period for that eternity in which man must dwell either in incredible bliss or indescribable horror. His chief business was to avoid the latter and attain the former. And the methods used were largely supernatural methods; that is, methods whereby men

> 66 [T]his naturalistic attitude toward the universe and this humanistic attitude toward human life leads to an entirely new type of religion, which perhaps is best described as naturalistic Humanism, and which involves a very definitely changed attitude and a very definite world-view. 99

Exhibit 12
1933

A Humanist Manifesto

1933

❝ The time has come for widespread recognition of the radical changes in religious beliefs. . . . In every field of human activity, the vital movement is now in the direction of a candid and explicit human- ism . . . religious humanism. **❞**

Note: These excerpts of *Humanist Manifesto I* are reprinted from Charles Francis Potter's book *Humanizing Religion* (New York: Harper & Brothers Publishers, 1933). The manifesto first appeared in *The New Humanist*, May/ June 1933 (Vol. VI, No. 3).

◄◄◄◄◄◄◄◄◄◄◄◄   (6)   ◄◄◄◄◄◄◄◄◄◄◄◄

A Humanist Manifesto

The time has come for widespread recognition of the radical changes in religious beliefs throughout the modern world. The time is past for mere revision of traditional attitudes. Science and economic change have disrupted the old beliefs. Religions the world over are under the necessity of coming to terms with new conditions created by a vastly increased knowledge and experience. In every field of human activity, the vital movement is now in the direction of a candid and explicit human- ism. In order that religious humanism may be better understood we, the undersigned, desire to make certain affirmations which we believe the facts of our contemporary life demonstrate.

There is great danger of a final, and we be- lieve fatal, identification of the word *religion* with doctrines and methods which have lost their significance and which are powerless to solve the problem of human living in the Twentieth Century. Religions have always been

The *Humanist Manifesto I* consistently describes Humanism as a religion. The signatories of this document believed that "to establish such a religion [Humanism] is a major necessity of the present." Most understood that the best way to establish this new religion was to control the education of the next generation.

““There is a great danger of a final, and we believe fatal, identification of the word *religion* with [traditional] doctrines and methods. . . . But through all changes religion itself remains constant in its quest for abiding values. . .””

means for realizing the highest values of life. Their end has been accomplished through the interpretation of the total environing situation (theology or world view), the sense of values resulting therefrom (goal or ideal), and the technique (cult) established for realizing the satisfactory life. A change in any of these factors results in alteration of the outward forms of religion. This fact explains the changefulness of religions through the centuries. But through all changes religion itself remains constant in its quest for abiding values, and inseparable feature of human life.

Today man's larger understanding of the universe, his scientific achievements, and his deeper appreciation of brotherhood, have created a situation which requires a new statement of the means and purposes of religion. Such a vital, fearless, and frank religion capable of furnishing adequate social goals and personal satisfactions may appear to many people as a complete break with the past. While this age does owe a vast debt to the traditional religions, it is none the less obvious that any religion that can hope to be a synthesizing and dynamic force for today

must be shaped for the needs of this age. To establish such a religion is a major necessity of the present. It is a responsibility which rests upon this generation. We therefore affirm the following:

First: Religious humanists regard the universe as self-existing and not created.

Second: Humanism believes that man is a part of nature and that he has emerged as the result of a continuous process.

Third: Holding an organic view of life, humanists find that the traditional dualism of mind and body must be rejected.

Fourth: Humanism recognizes that man's religious culture and civilization, as clearly depicted by anthropology and history, are the product of a gradual development due to his interaction with his natural environment and with his social heritage. The individual born into a particular culture is largely moulded by that culture.

Fifth: Humanism asserts that the nature of the universe depicted by modern science makes unacceptable any supernatural or cosmic guarantees of human values. Obviously humanism

““To establish such a religion [humanism] is a major necessity of the present.””

Exhibit 13

HUMANIZING RELIGION

BY

CHARLES FRANCIS POTTER

FOUNDER AND LEADER OF

THE FIRST HUMANIST SOCIETY OF NEW YORK

HARPER & BROTHERS PUBLISHERS
New York and London
1933

❝ . . . belief in a new religion called Humanism . . . ❞

❝[S]omething of more than ordinary importance in religious circles has occurred.❞

▶▶▶▶▶▶▶▶▶▶▶▶ (1) ◀◀◀◀◀◀◀◀◀◀◀◀◀◀

*The Recent Rise of
Religious Humanism*

WHEN eleven eminent professors of philosophy, theology, economics, medicine, and sociology, and twenty-three other leaders in editorial, literary, educational, and religious fields come out publicly over their own signatures and confess to belief in a new religion called Humanism, and state fifteen theses upon which they all agree, then something of more than ordinary importance in religious circles has occurred. The fact that these men come from various denominational and religious backgrounds, including Unitarianism, Universalism, Judaism, and Ethical Culture, increases the significance of the new movement.

The Humanist Manifesto, signed by these men and printed in a summarized form in an Associated Press dispatch in the newspapers of the United States on May 1, 1933, was the first intimation received by many persons of the existence of such a movement, but it has been

Charles Francis Potter argues that modern Humanism is a religious movement with deep Unitarian roots. He authored *Humanism: A New Religion* and was a signatory of *Humanist Manifesto I*.

> ❝ Dr. John H. Dietrich . . . has been consistently setting forth the Humanist view in religion . . . ❞

quietly spreading for more than a decade and has for some time been a very lively topic of discussion in religious circles.

Dr. John H. Dietrich, minister of the First Unitarian Society of Minneapolis, is usually credited with being the "dean" of the Humanists, for he has been consistently setting forth the Humanist view in religion for at least eighteen years. His published sermons in six volumes, besides scores in pamphlet form, have been an important factor in the spread of the new faith.

Dr. Curtis W. Reese, of Abraham Lincoln Center, Chicago, has been preaching Humanism for nearly, if not quite, as long, and has written *Humanism*, 1926, and *Humanist Religion*, 1931, besides editing in 1927 a volume of *Humanist Sermons* by eighteen preachers.

Dr. Albert C. Dieffenbach, for fifteen years the aggressive and able editor of the Unitarian weekly, the *Christian Register*, has done much to give Humanism a fair hearing in liberal circles.

Indeed, it is among Unitarian ministers that Humanism has spread most rapidly, so that

the denomination is probably now to be classed as one third Humanist, one third Theist, and the remaining third "on the fence."

As a separate movement, without affiliation with even the Unitarian denomination, the rise of Humanism dates from 1929 when The Hollywood Humanist Society was founded by Rev. Theodore Curtis Abell, and The First Humanist Society of New York by the present writer. In the current year, 1933, separate Humanist societies have been established in Sioux City, Iowa, by Rev. Gordon Kent, and in Berkeley, California, by Rev. Eldred C. Vanderlaan.

In January, 1930, five university professors led by Dr. Jesse H. Holmes of Swarthmore College, prominent in Quaker circles, sent several thousand letters throughout the country urging a modernization of Christianity so radical as to arrive practically at the Humanist position.

The trend toward Humanism is so marked among the representatives of all the more liberal groups of Christianity and Judaism that it will probably be only a matter of time, and a brief time at that, before Humanism will be

> ❝ Indeed, it is among Unitarian ministers that Humanism has spread most rapidly. ❞

generally recognized as the logical faith of those whose modern point of view forces them to abandon the inevitable supernaturalism of the theistic position.

The large proportion of university professors among the signers of the manifesto reveals that there exists among the educated classes of this country a widespread attitude of protest amounting practically to rebellion against organized Christianity, and that the complacent theism of the churches no longer supplies satisfactory mental food to the thinkers of the land.

Some readers were surprised to discover among the signers of the manifesto the name of Dr. John Dewey, who is generally reckoned, especially in other countries, as perhaps our leading philosopher and educator. But Dr. Dewey has long been sympathetic in his attitude toward Humanism. In the *Thinker* of June, 1930, he corrected a common misapprehension, when he stated,—

The new religious movement that calls itself Humanism does not propose to worship humanity, much less set up a system of rites which are to do

> " [I]t will probably be only a matter of time, and a brief time at that, before Humanism will be generally recognized as the logical faith . . . "

for this worship what the sacraments did for medieval Christianity. It finds its conceptions of God and of other religious ideas of the past in the realm of human ideals and aspirations, and would yoke the religious emotions of mankind to the promotion of the ideal phases of human life. . . .

At all events, what Humanism means to me is an expansion, not a contraction, of human life, an expansion in which nature and the science of nature are made the willing servants of human good.

> " The new religious movement that calls itself Humanism . . . finds its conceptions of God and of other religious ideas of the past in the realm of human ideals and aspirations . . . "

Exhibit 14

1934

A
COMMON FAITH
JOHN DEWEY

NEW HAVEN AND LONDON
YALE UNIVERSITY PRESS

1934

❝Here are all the elements for a religious faith that shall not be confined to sect, class, or race.**❞**

THE HUMAN ABODE   87

of practical faith in ideal ends is positive and outreaching.

The considerations put forward in the present chapter may be summed up in what they imply. The ideal ends to which we attach our faith are not shadowy and wavering. They assume concrete form in our understanding of our relations to one another and the values contained in these relations. We who now live are parts of a humanity that extends into the remote past, a humanity that has interacted with nature. The things in civilization we most prize are not of ourselves. They exist by grace of the doings and sufferings of the continuous human community in which we are a link. Ours is the responsibility of conserving, transmitting, rectifying and expanding the heritage of values we have received that those who come after us may receive it more solid and secure, more widely accessible and more generously shared than we have received it. Here are all the elements for a religious faith that shall not be confined to sect, class, or race. Such a faith has always been implicitly the common faith of mankind. It remains to make it explicit and militant.

John Dewey delivered his Terry Lectures at Yale University in 1933, and later published them in *A Common Faith*. Dewey helped establish the American Civil Liberties Union and the League for Industrial Democracy, and was the first president of the American Association of University Professors.

Exhibit 15

1936

AMERICAN PHILOSOPHIES OF RELIGION

BY

HENRY NELSON WIEMAN
Professor of Philosophy of Religion
The University of Chicago

BERNARD EUGENE MELAND
Professor of Religion and Philosophy
Central College, Fayette, Missouri

WILLETT, CLARK & COMPANY
CHICAGO   NEW YORK
1936

“The form of religious humanism . . . is best represented in philosophic literature by M.C. Otto, R.W. Sellars and A.E. Haydon.”

258   American Philosophies of Religion

becomes a very inadequate guide to the understanding of religion if one shares his supposition that all religion is a compensatory illusion; for that assumption overlooks the fact that religion, like every other important human interest, manifests itself both in pathological and in salutary forms. Martin has ignored the normal, healthy expressions of religion and has restricted his analysis to pathological behavior, identifying it with religion as a whole. This is his inadequacy. Yet it must be admitted that he has presented a strikingly clear analysis of pathological religion. However invalid the psychological basis of his analysis, he has called attention to the important fact of the pathological expression of religion. The importance of this is that it opens the way to clearing up the ambiguities that have accumulated in theologies and philosophies of religion concerning the nature and function of religion. Strange to say, there has been little or no conscious distinction among theologians and philosophers, in determining religious values and their criteria, between the sources issuing from pathological experience and those growing out of normal healthy religious living. Before religion can become a dependable spiritual quest, its objectives and insights must be extricated from the realm of the pathological.[5]

RELIGIOUS HUMANISM

The form of religious humanism, arising out of the broader socio-historical field, is best represented in philosophic literature by M. C. Otto, R. W. Sellars and A. E. Haydon. As a religious movement, its prominent representatives are John H. Dietrich, Curtis W. Reese, John Haynes Holmes, Charles F. Potter, J. A. C. F. Auer, L. M. Birkhead, Burdette Backus, Oliver Reiser, Harold Buschman, R.B. Bragg, Edwin H. Wilson, and a host of others whose names appear as signatures to the Humanist Manifesto.

As a theory of religion, religious humanism may be said to be the culmination of the gradual shift in theological and phil-

Henry Wieman and Bernard Meland include "Religious Humanism" in their discussion of American philosophies of religion. Wieman, a signatory of *Humanist Manifesto I*, later identifies himself as an empirical theist.

" As a theory of religion, religious humanism may be said to be the culmination of the gradual shift in theological and philosophical thinking from the God-ward to the man-ward side of religious thought. **"**

{ osophical thinking from the God-ward to the man-ward side of religious thought.[6] This shift has come about under the stimulus of two lines of reasoning: One group of thinkers has insisted that the objective, or God-ward side, being simply the projection of man's own wish and idealization, is non-existent, except as it exists in man's own consciousness. Another group, believing that the objective aspect has been stressed to the point of obscuring, if not eclipsing utterly, the vital interests of the human enterprise, has urged a concerted emphasis upon the human aspect. Humanists who have held to the first point of view have been antitheistic. Those who have taken the second stand have varied in the degree of their acceptance of a belief in God, but their views have not been necessarily hostile to theism in theory. In most cases they have chosen simply to ignore the theistic aspect so as to see clearly the full implications and possibilities of man and his powers.

In considering the subjectivist theories of religion, particularly the view advanced by Feuerbach, we came upon a mode of thought leading to the first type of humanism. A more directly contributive forerunner to the contemporary movement of religious humanism is the philosophy of Positivism, developed by the French philosophers Saint-Simon and Auguste Comte in the nineteenth century. Contemporary religious humanism is not to be viewed as a direct outgrowth of Positivism, however. It is more than a philosophical movement. At the core, it is a social passion, arising from two convictions: one, that within the world of nature itself there is no guarantor of human values, and second, that the control of nature through the technological sciences is fraught with both blessedness and peril, but that to date its efforts, as evidenced in the rise of our machine civilization, the development of instruments of war, and the economic structure that promote both, is heavily weighted on the side of peril. In the face of this growing catastrophe, the religious humanists have turned from philosophical speculation and religious worship, as they formerly

Exhibit 16

1937

MAN'S SEARCH FOR
THE GOOD LIFE ➤ An
Inquiry into the Nature of
Religions ➤ ➤ ➤ ➤ ➤
By A. EUSTACE HAYDON

HARPER & BROTHERS *Publishers*
New York *and* London ➤ ➤ 1937

Contents

A. Eustace Haydon, a signatory of *Humanist Manifesto I*, believed that man must develop a religion for modern times—Humanism. When he speaks of "the task of religion," he is speaking of the task of Humanism.

> "Modern religion will use the method of science and the techniques of all the sciences to secure a progressive realization of man's ever-changing desires.
>
> The task of religion is to make the shared quest for the good life the controlling, unifying center of the human, life process."

techniques were twofold—some for practical, material ends, some for the realization of spiritual values. With greater control over physical goods the practical technique drew away from the ceremonial in some cultures. Modern religion will use the method of science and the techniques of all the sciences to secure a progressive realization of man's ever-changing desires.

The task of religion is to make the shared quest for the good life the controlling, unifying center of the human, life process. All the history of the world rings the changes upon this theme. All the ages have followed it as a moving star over the horizon of every generation. All theologies and religious philosophies have been ways of reading the ideal into the ultimate structure of the universe. All the gods have served this vision. All religions have kept the faith in a final realization of the hope. Through all man's history one thing has been lacking—the effective, practical method of making the vision of a shared life take on the form of actuality. The task remains to test the intelligence of this generation. Men have been loyal through all the ages to the ideal, but loyalty is not enough. Great souls in all cultures have dared to

[254]

THE RETURN TO EARTH

defy the forces of evil and die for the cause of man, but dying is not enough. Dreamers have scaled the bleak mountains of despair and challenged the heavens with unshaken faith, but faith is not enough. Wherever evils have crushed the lives of men, where sorrow has broken their hearts or injustice destroyed their spirits, there have been devoted ones to play the Samaritan part and bind up the wounds of the sufferers, but devotion is not enough.

The task demands a mobilization of intelligence to give religion embodiment in a culture which will make the values of an abundant life available to all men. The divisive wills and selfish interests of groups and nations must bow before the one human purpose if civilization is to be cured of its historic drifting through waste and disaster. The intelligence of men, devoted to the human cause, must develop a major strategy—a program that will enlist the knowledge, training, and power necessary to transmute the dream of faith into concrete reality. It will mean the use of all available methods for the analysis of human relations to discover satisfying solutions for social maladjustments, the coordination of all scattered efforts of ameliora-

[255]

> "The task demands a mobilization of intelligence to give religion embodiment in a culture which will make the values of an abudant life available to all men. . . . a program that will enlist the knowledge, training, and power necessary to transmute the dream of faith into concrete reality."

Exhibit 17

1946

HUMANISM—A RELIGION FOR SCIENTISTS }

By ARCHIE J. BAHM

DEPARTMENT OF PHILOSOPHY AND SOCIOLOGY, TEXAS TECHNOLOGICAL COLLEGE

OPPOSITION of science and religion seems sensible to some and absurd to others; which view one holds depends in part upon what one means by religion. If religion is defined as consisting of traditional dogmas and the ecclesiastical systems interested in maintaining them, then the view that science and religion are opposed may well be justified. But if religion be conceived as faith in the worth-whileness of living and active pursuit of what seems worth while, then science and religion are not opposed and science is a very important part of religion.

Narrow religionists and narrow scientists alike agree that each is opposed to the other, but broad religionists and broad scientists recognize that science and religion involve each other. It is said that science deals with facts and religion with values. This is true, but it is not the whole truth. For there are facts about values and vice versa.

As for facts about values, it is a fact that values exist; that they are what they are; and that they are experienceable. Values, as observable data, are open to scientific investigation, and it is a sad commentary on science that such investigation has been so long neglected by so many of those who have faith in science.

As for values about facts, if facts were of no value, scientists would not be interested in them, and if they were not useful, no one would ever become a scientist. Even those "pure" scientists who seek "facts for their own sake" seek values, because for their own sake means that the values are self-contained. Thus science is pursuit of values as well as of facts.

If religion is the comprehensive name for pursuit of values, then science, insofar as it is pursuit of values, is a part of religion. This conclusion is so unsatisfactory to those scientists who are in the habit of thinking of religion in terms of traditional dogmas that some explanation of the "true" nature of religion seems desirable, that is, of that view of the nature of religion which one would reach if he investigated the matter scientifically. In other words, the investigator should be open-minded, tolerant, willing to be guided by experience and reason, and without prejudgment as to what the conclusion will be. Some scientists who maintain such an attitude toward problems within their field fail to do so in other fields, and the difficulty they have in maintaining a scientific attitude in the field of religion, or with respect to values, is so great that they have come to insist that science cannot deal with values and, by implication, with facts about values. But other scientists have faith in the applicability of scientific attitudes to facts about values and have sought to make a scientific approach to religion.

The scientific investigator will make extended and careful observation of data, classify data into types based on similarities and differences, formulate hypotheses about the nature of the data, and verify hypotheses by applying them to additional data. In seeking to understand religion the scientist observes extensively whatever is called religion by different people at different times; he examines hypotheses which others have held as well as those suggested by his own surveys; and he tests all these hypotheses to discover their relative merits in inter-

310

Scientific Monthly April, 1946

Archie J. Bahm, a signatory of *Humanist Manifesto II*, argues that science and religion can mix, as long as the religion is Secular Humanism.

"HUMANISM—A RELIGION FOR SCIENTISTS"

" [I]f religion be conceived as faith in the worth-whileness of living and active pursuit of what seems worth while, then science and religion are not opposed and science is a very important part of religion. "

Exhibit 18

1952

RELIGION IN 20TH CENTURY AMERICA

HERBERT WALLACE SCHNEIDER

HARVARD UNIVERSITY PRESS

CAMBRIDGE, MASSACHUSETTS

1952

"Intellectually humanism has not yet achieved an orthodoxy of its own, though humanist creeds are being circulated, and a "fourth faith" is in the making.**"**

INTELLECTUAL RECONSTRUCTION   141

thought has progressed further than among Christians. The Reconstructionist Movement which the Society for the Advancement of Judaism has promoted combines the historical, philosophical, and social aspects of Judaism in a remarkable and radical way. But being specifically a theory of Jewish civilization and national aspirations, it is not directly applicable to a more universal theology, except as an illustration of method; and, besides, the rabbis are far from agreed as to how far this kind of reconstruction can be carried without being destructive.

The New Humanism

One more phase of the critique of liberalism must be mentioned to round out our account of the present intellectual situation. A minority of the liberals, their modernist wing, has concluded from the course of events that liberalism fell into disrepute because it was not liberal enough, because it made compromises all along the line: compromises with theism, with nationalism, with supernaturalism, with ecclesiastical politics, and with sectarian interests. To them the chief enemies of free religion are the flight from reason, the defense of historical creeds, the institutionalization of faith, and the lack of fraternal respect among religions. Discouraged by the revival of theology and intolerance among religious bodies, these modernists from many faiths have banded together under the banner of humanism. Though they are trying desperately not to become one more sect, and therefore are cultivating an informal fellowship among humanists of many religions, they are inevitably becoming militant and are organizing for missionary activity. Intellectually humanism has not yet achieved an orthodoxy of its own, though humanist creeds are being circulated, and a "fourth faith" is in the making. In *A Humanist Manifesto*, first published in 1933 but still used by the group as an anticreedal creed, the most striking affirmation is the seventh, containing the following definition of religion:

Religion consists of those actions, purposes, and experiences which are humanly significant. Nothing human is alien to the religious. It includes labor, art, science, philosophy, love, friendship, recreation— all that is in its degree expressive of intelligently satisfying human living. The distinction between the sacred and the secular can no longer be maintained.

Herbert Wallace Schneider was a signatory of *Humanist Manifesto II*. In *Religion in 20th Century America*, Schneider explains that "it is necessary to recognize that secularism or its equivalent exists as a positive faith."

> ❝The reappearance of humanism as an independent religious movement is significant in spite of its small numbers.❞

Though this statement could readily be criticized as a definition of religion, it serves admirably, as most creeds do, not to define religion in general but to exhibit the import of a particular faith. Basic to this faith is the attempt to substitute for the distinction between the sacred and the secular, the distinction between the humane and the inhumane.

There are among the humanists left-wing Unitarians who reflect the liberalism of Emerson and who like him do not wish to be confined to Christian limitations. There are materialists who are no longer "doctrinaire" materialists, but who are suspicious of theologians who use terms like "soul," "immortal," "transcendental," "God," and "Spirit"; they prefer more secular language for more secular truths. There are naturalists who are disgusted by the sophisticated use of supernaturalist symbols and myths among neo-radical theologians, who find no use for organized religions, but who have a "religious" concern for the life of reason. There are still a few old-fashioned rationalists, freethinkers, or professional atheists, who mourn the failure of humanitarianism as a universal religion, and who are therefore willing to call themselves religious humanists. There are many liberal spirits in the ranks of Christian churches, Judaism, Ethical Culture, and other distinctive religious bodies, who resent the exclusiveness of their organizations and join the humanist fellowship in order to bear witness to their personal, broader faith. And there are many individuals who cannot be labeled, since they do not feel at home either in any religious body or in the cold world of secular interests; nevertheless they seek some expression for their passionate desire to promote "the complete realization of human personality" and "a free and universal society." The humanist societies have succeeded in bringing these various kinds of liberals together for fellowship, instruction, publication, and promotion of their common interests. The reappearance of humanism as an independent religious movement is significant in spite of its small numbers. It gives proof through the night that modernist liberalism still lives as a positive religious faith, that the demand for religious expression exceeds the supply offered by conventional religious bodies, and that philosophers are not as hopelessly individualistic as they appear to be to more conformist

minds. Those who share the comforts of a conventional religious home are continually confronted in a free country with free religion. Though freethinkers are apt to appear as religious orphans or vagabonds to those whose intellectual lives are more comfortable and sociable, these free spirits in their wanderings and seekings produce their fair share of prophets, and usually serve the causes of enlightenment and brotherhood which no religion worthy of the name would now dare to deny, since all are ashamed when they betray them.

There exists also in a form less organized and evident than the religious humanist movement a significant number of religious secularists. For them secularism represents neither irreligion nor religious indifference, but a positive concern (as near to "absolute" concern as they dare come) for certain values and institutions, which they wish to defend as sacred, if necessary, against all organized religion. They regard themselves as the champions of democracy, freedom, and science, and they often appeal to the spirit of Thomas Jefferson as their American patron saint. They are usually anticlericals and believe that it is possible to express a "common faith" to which all free spirits are loyal and which unites those whom organized religion divides.

How many reformers and prophets have suffered persecution and martyrdom in their efforts to do away with the cramping survivals of religious infantilism! How childish do the trappings of orthodoxy seem to the mature mind! How eagerly do the traditionalists and the fundamentalists cling to the doctrines and forms of religion which have lost their power to enlist the hearty support of modern man! Is it not high time that we unite in the endeavor to define and practice a religion of adults?[26]

Horace M. Kallen has given an able and representative expression of such a religion in his *Of Clericalism and Secularism in Religion.*[27] For how many of the approximately 30 per cent of Americans who are religiously "unaffiliated" he speaks it is difficult to say. But it is necessary to recognize that secularism or its equivalent exists as a positive faith, that it is not necessarily "Godless," though unorganized and theologically inarticulate, and that it is not religiously illiterate. It is strongly represented among the literary intelligentsia, in political circles, among social scientists

> ❝There exists also in a form less organized and evident than the religious humanist movement a significant number of religious secularists. . . . [I]t is necessary to recognize that secularism or its equivalent exists as a positive faith. . . .❞

Exhibit 19

1953

*The religion
of a chemist
and Humanist*

What Can We Believe?

HAROLD R. RAFTON

What can we believe? Many answers have been given to this question: we here present the answer of Humanism. For those unfamiliar with Humanism it may be pointed out that Humanism down the centuries has had many meanings. Perhaps the best known usage is that signifying the return to the classics of Greece and Rome in the Middle Ages —the revolt against the sterility of scholasticism which was among the first stirrings of the Renaissance. More recently it has signified a school of literature of which Professor Irving Babbitt of Harvard was a leader. But the Humanism in which we are interested is different from any of these. Although it is rooted far in the past, beginning with some early Greek philosophers, its present embodiment had its origin largely in the thought of two Unitarian ministers, Curtis Reese and John Dietrich, some thirty years or so ago. It is a philosophy of naturalism, centered in man, based on the findings of science, and employing the scientific method. It is sometimes called "religious Humanism" to signify that it operates in the religious field.

As interpreted by the Humanist Fellowship of Boston and formulated in its by-laws:

"Humanism is a religion dedicated to the ennoblement and enrichment of human life through human effort, in accordance with the methods and findings of science and the growing wisdom of man.

"Humanism, on the basis of the evidence now available, considers that nature is all-embracing; that man is a part of, and the only personality in, nature, and was evolved by natural processes; and that man is responsible for his own progress and can look to this life alone for the fulfillment of his aspirations."

These are generalizations, and for persons of traditional religious background it may be helpful to examine familiar religious terminology and see how the concepts of Humanism correspond to or differ therefrom. Comment will be confined to the more important religious terms, as an exhaustive consideration is obviously beyond the scope of this article. Humanists have no official creed, no authoritarian rule, and therefore it would be presumptuous for me to attempt to set up a standard for the belief of Humanists; so it should be understood that I am presenting my personal conception of Humanism, and where I use the word "we," or speak of "Humanists," I do so in the editorial sense.

Perhaps the most important characteristic of the traditional religions is belief in a supreme being. Do Humanists believe in a supreme being? Emphatically yes. That supreme being is man. Humanists have no knowledge of any being more supreme.

Page 118

THE HUMANIST

men. Because experience has shown that the greatest satisfaction is derived from service rather than self-seeking. Humanists stress the ideal of service. As the basis of our ethic we place the welfare of the human community first, but we believe this is best served by the greatest freedom of the individual consistent with the common good.

Happiness is our aim, not only for ourselves, but for all mankind. The welfare of our fellows is our concern. We know no cosmic love—but we have experienced human love, and we seek to expand affection, fellowship and appreciation to the widest circles.

Humanism does not claim to know all the answers to current problems, but it considers it fatuous to apply outmoded primitive religious concepts to the atomic age. It uses instead the scientific method, the only one which has so far proved reliable for the acquisition of knowledge and understanding. Humanism is striving to cope with our problems with the insight of reason, tempered by fellowship, illumined by love.

That Humanists have much to learn, we freely admit; and doubtless when people of the twenty-fifth century look back upon us they will think some of our present humanistic ideas naive in the light of their ripened wisdom, just as they will think our airplanes quaint in the light of their interplanetary ships. This, of course, is as we would have it, since we sincerely hope that religion, in common with all other areas of human thought, will continue to progress. But, as those living in a distant future look back at us with all our shortcomings, this, at least, we feel they will be able to say: *"In the twentieth century, in the field of religion, the Humanists were fully abreast of their times!"*

Because Humanists believe we have no outside power to help us, Humanists rely on human and natural resources. This fosters co-operation with our fellow

OOPS!

On page 79 of the No. 2, 1953, number you call The Golden Ass *"a satiracal comedy written in the late middle ages." It is not a comedy, but that does not matter: what is important is that Apuleius's dates are 125-200 A.D., and the book was written before 155—which is hardly the middle ages, late or early.*

MRS. MAYNARD SHIPLEY

Page 124

THE HUMANIST

Harold A. Rafton, organizer and president of the Humanist Fellowship of Boston, Inc., published this essay in *The Humanist,* 1953, Number 3. Although Humanists purport to despise dogma, they preach a dogmatic naturalism in response to the question, What can we believe?

1953

❝ As interpreted by the Humanist Fellowship of Boston and formulated in its by-laws:

"Humanism is a religion dedicated to the ennoblement and enrichment of human life through human effort, in accordance with the method and findings of science and the growing wisdom of man.

"Humanism, on the basis of the evidence now available, considers that nature is all-embracing; that man is a part of, and the only personality in, nature, and was evolved by natural processes; and that man is responsible for his own progress and can look to this life alone for the fulfillment of his aspirations." **❞**

❝ Perhaps the most important characteristic of the traditional religions is belief in a supreme being. Do Humanists believe in a supreme being? Emphatically yes. That supreme being is man. Humanists have no knowledge of any being more supreme. **❞**

❝ But, as those living in a distant future look back at us with all our shortcomings, this, at least, we feel they will be able to say: *"In the twentieth century, in the field of religion, the Humanists were fully abreast of their times!"* **❞**

64

Exhibit 20

1953

[The Humanist]

"I have read the comments [of the other original signers] in the proofs, and I really have nothing to add to them.

"It may be that a new Humanist declaration is desirable, as indicated in several of the comments, but my own feeling is that the original one may well stand, for is it likely that there could be agreement upon anything better?

"In any case, I feel no interest in a revision of the Humanist Manifesto."

—Albert C. Dieffenbach, *Cambridge, Massachusetts*

"I do not have a copy of the Manifesto at hand, so cannot comment on it in detail, but I think you are wise to let it stand as an historical document. It is definitely a dated instrument and represents what I have come to feel is a dated philosophy—a philosophy too narrow in its conception of great cosmic schemes, about which we know so little, and concerning which we should be less dogmatic and arrogant. It in no wise reflects the humility which becomes the real seeker after truth. But that is the kind of fellows we were in those days. In fact, I was one of the chief offenders, and I confess it now in all humility. I see now that my utter reliance upon science and reason and my contempt for any intuitive insights and intangible values, which are the very essence of art and religion, was a great mistake. I think the Humanism of that period served a good purpose as a protest movement, but its day is passed. What I am trying to say is that the positive side of Humanism was and is fine—its insistence upon the enrichment of life in its every form; but its negative side, cutting itself off from all cosmic relationship, and denying or ignoring every influence outside of humanity itself, I think, was and is very shortsighted."

—John H. Dietrich, *Berkely, California*

"I believe that the Humanist Manifesto of 1933 was a landmark in the development of religious and philosophical Humanism. It is an historical document of great worth and importance in the Humanist movement and must be included as vital source material in any careful study of modern Humanism. Frank criticism of the Manifesto, however, must be the prelude to any new declaration of basic Humanist principles.

"In my opinion the Humanist Manifesto's definition of religion is far too vague; and for this reason I would favor the omission of Point Seven altogether. In its place, in the preface, I suggest some such definition as this: 'Religion is an integrated and inclusive way of life to which a group of persons give supreme commitment and which involves the shared quest of the ideal.' At the same time I would not repeat the phrase 'religious humanism' throughout the Manifesto, but would talk merely of 'Humanism.' In the preface, too, should be a statement that Humanism is 'a religion or philosophy.'

"The First Point of the Manifesto I would rephrase as follows: 'Humanism regards the universe as eternal, self-existing and uncreated, with no supernatural origins or destiny. This universe is dynamic in its very structure and is constantly changing in its every aspect.'

"To the Second Point I would add this sentence: 'Man's inseparable unity of mind and body indicates that in all probability there is no personal survival after death.'

"Point Six should be revised as out of date, with 'the several varieties of neo-orthodoxy' substituted for 'modernism and the several varieties of new thought.'

"Point Fourteen, as I have been saying for many years, goes too far in involving Humanism in fundamental economic issues. Humanism as such should not claim to have solutions for all human problems or set itself up as a specific economics, political science, or sociology. In place of Point Fourteen, I think a new declaration

This page contains a few responses to questions regarding *Humanist Manifesto I.* The key paragraph is part of the response written by Corliss Lamont, a leader of the Humanist movement and a signatory of *Humanist Manifesto II.* Lamont authored many works on Humanism, including *The Philosophy of Humanism.* He financially supported the Harvard University Humanist Chaplain (see Exhibit 45).

“ In my opinion the Humanist Manifesto's definition of religion is far too vague; and for this reason I would favor the omission of Point Seven altogether. In its place, in the preface, I suggest some such definition as this: 'Religion is an integrated and inclusive way of life to which a group of persons give supreme commitment and which involves the shared quest of the ideal.' At the same time I would not repeat the phrase 'religious humanism' throughout the Manifesto, but would talk merely of 'Humanism.' In the preface, too, should be a statement that Humanism is 'a religion or philosophy.' ”

Corliss Lamont

Exhibit 21

1954

" *The Fourth Faith* **"**

HUMANISM
AS THE NEXT STEP

An Introduction
for Liberal Protestants, Catholics, and Jews

By LLOYD *and* MARY MORAIN

THE BEACON PRESS · BOSTON

[1954]

CHAPTER ONE

The Fourth Faith

A Growing Movement

4   HUMANISM AS THE NEXT STEP

In Islam: "No one of you is a believer until he desires for his brother that which he desires for himself" (*Sunnah*).

In Judaism: "What is hateful to you, do not to your fellowman. That is the entire Law; all the rest is commentary" (*Talmud, Shabbat* 31*d*).

In Taoism: "Regard your neighbor's gain as your own gain, and your neighbor's loss as your own loss" (*T'ai Shang Kan Ying P'ien*).

Upon this common ethical basis have been built varying religious practices and diverse theological beliefs.

Down through the ages men have been seeking a universal religion or way of life. They are still seeking. Throughout the world there are wide cultural variations. Ways of worship, rituals, symbols, and sacraments are different. Humanism, built squarely on the universal idea of brotherhood, upon the golden rule, shows promise of becoming a great world faith.

Humanists are content with fixing their attention on this life and on this earth. Theirs is a religion without a God, divine revelation, or sacred scriptures. Yet theirs is a faith rich in feeling and understanding. They see sorrows and joys, tragedies and triumphs, touching every fiber of human life. They experience wholesome humility as they venture forward with their fellow men into the as-yet-unknown.

We may now note several facts about this rapidly growing philosophy and religion.

(1) It has developed in response to the spiritual needs and aspirations of people in different parts of the world.

(2) It contains an ethical core similar to that of many religions and philosophies.

" Humanists are content with fixing their attention on this life and on this earth. Theirs is a religion without a God, divine revelation, or sacred scriptures. Yet theirs is a faith rich in feeling and understanding. **"**

Both Lloyd and Mary Morain are signatories of *Humanist Manifesto II*. Lloyd is a former president of the American Humanist Association. In 1994 he and his wife were designated Humanists of the Year. The Morains view Humanism as the Fourth Faith, and the next great world religion.

> **[Humanism] is a philosophy of men's relations to one another and to nature, rather than of men's relations to deity.**

> **Julian Huxley. . .is among those who believe that humanism will be the world's next great faith.**

1954

(3) It is free from divisive doctrines about the unknown, deity, revelation, sacred scriptures, rituals, sacraments, formal theology, and such befuddling ideas as the radical separation of either the world or the individual into matter and spirit.

(4) It is a philosophy of men's relations to one another and to nature, rather than of men's relations to deity.

Built on this fresh, vital basis it is little wonder that humanism has called forth accelerated world-wide interest. In 1952, for the first time, representatives from humanist groups in many countries met in Holland and formed the International Humanist and Ethical Union. Julian Huxley, a biologist and the first Director-General of Unesco, served as president. He is among those who believe that humanism will be the world's next great faith.

Here in the United States the number of humanist groups has doubled in each of the past several years. Some of these groups, for example, many of the Unitarian Fellowships, are functioning under the auspices of a liberal religious denomination. Each year more and more Protestants, Catholics, and Jews, as well as many without any previous religious affiliation, are coming to follow as their own this way of life.

This faith is held by a large number of individuals who have made or are making solid contributions to human welfare and understanding. Among distinguished humanists of the recent past are Edwin G. Conklin, John Dewey, Horace Fries, John Galsworthy, Frederick J. Gould, Sir Richard Gregory, John A. Hobson, James H. Leuba, Sinclair Lewis, Eduard C. Lindeman, F. S. Marvin, Arthur B. Moehlman, Hans Reichenbach, Porter Sargent, and George Santayana. Their influence has spread in

One of the great religious humanist pioneers, John Dietrich, pointed out:

For centuries the idea of God has been the very heart of religion; it has been said "no God, no religion." But humanism thinks of religion as something very different and far deeper than any belief in God. To it, religion is not the attempt to establish right relations with a supernatural being, but rather the upreaching and aspiring impulse in a human life. It is life striving for its completest fulfillment, and anything which contributes to this fulfillment is religious, whether it be associated with the idea of God or not.

Another humanist pioneer, Charles Francis Potter, defines humanism as, "Faith in the supreme self-perfectibility of the human personality."

Humanism gives to many people the satisfactions which have come to them in the past either from other religions or from other philosophies. In doing this it serves some as a religion, others as a philosophy. Inasmuch as it is both a philosophy and a religion there is no need to deny that it has both functions.

It developed as the scientific viewpoint was grafted upon a philosophy of good will and of confidence in men and nature. It is neither vague nor colorless but positive and dynamic, whether thought of as a religion, a philosophy, or a way of life.

> **Inasmuch as [Humanism] is both a philosophy and a religion there is no need to deny that it has both functions.**

Exhibit 22
1955

*Ideals and symbols
of a
democratic religion*

The Religion of Democracy
Part II
RUDOLF DREIKURS

III. Aspects of the Next Great Religion

The "spiritual needs" of mankind do not require supernatural concepts; they merely constitute a need for an orientation which can lift individuals out of the daily tribulations and provide perspectives *sub specie aeternitatis*, under the aspects of eternity. A new society will need its own religion because society needs orientation, crystallization of its concepts and perspectives, of its morals and values.

To be sure, this new and universal religion does not exist as yet. Nobody can say what it will be like. But certain aspects of the future democratic religion are becoming clear. Let us consider a few of them.

1. *The new religion will probably be humanistic.* It will be concerned with man and not with God. The concept of a personal God, of a power outside of our natural experience, of supernatural forces, does not fit a scientifically oriented way of life of individuals who become aware of their independence and self-determination, of their strength and force within themselves.

A new picture of the world, and of man in it, emerges through the newest scientific discoveries. Self-determination and inner freedom become recognized as an intrinsic part of all existence, including inorganic matter. Man is discovering that all this strength and power which inspire his awe when he beholds a thunderstorm, a raging stream or waterfall, a snowcapped mountain in all its majesty, that this power of life not only surrounds and threatens him from without; but it is within him

Page 266   THE HUMANIST

> ❝The new religion will probably be humanistic. It will be concerned with man and not with God.❞

and is at his own personal disposal. Each individual human being, with all his tremendous abilities and power, also deserves a comparable awe and admiration because of his intricate biological functioning as well as his complex mental and emotional capacities. Man is a creator; he does not merely react to whatever may impress him, he acts and moves actively. The powers around him cannot be divided into supreme or less supreme powers. Within himself and about him he is confronted with life and has to find a way of meeting it satisfactorily. That is the essence of a humanistic orientation in regard to the universe.

2. *Religious truth will be scientific truth.* But this truth will be of fundamentally different nature than previous generations and cultures could ever have visualized. There is no longer an absolute truth. Absolutes exist only in an autocracy where a power has established itself to dictate what is truth. Truth is reality, but man can perceive reality only in a limited way. Therefore, he can only find approximations to truth, but not the absolute, not the *Ding an Sich* of Kant. Relativity replaces absolutes.

But within this restricted field of the knowable, scientific research and not revelation can provide information. And what we can know is sufficient to permit adequate living so that we do not have to concern ourselves with what we cannot know.

Only in a democratic era will the exploration of truth and scientific research be free. It never has been so in the past. Religious authorities or socially dominant groups restricted what could be known. Many Galilei are still sacrificed because their discoveries do not suit those who still have the power to control. The democratic religion will oppose such powers as the Christian religion opposes the devil. The interest of society is preserved by its religious concepts; the democratic society will develop religious concepts which guarantee the democratic process for the benefit of all.

3. *Religious prescriptions will serve new morals.* What the moral concepts of a democracy will be, nobody can say. New moral values are emerging with the present democratic evolution, and many time-honored traditional moral concepts are crumbling. A new society will require new moral regulations, different from a past cultural period. We are still enmeshed in the tradition of an autocratic past; therefore, we cannot visualize clearly the perspectives which eventually will emerge. Living

Later in this essay, Rudolph Dreikurs argues that the new religion (i.e. Humanism) will have new ideals, new symbols, and new rituals. In other words, both the *form* and the *content* of Humanism should be considered religious.

> ❝Such a new religion will be capable of combining the collective experience of the primitive society with the individual self-realization of civilization.❞

are more effective—or better, they alone are effective in our democratic atmosphere.

Today the symbol of the bad, if you want to call it "sin," is *fear*. Fear was an integral part of orthodox religion; it was used to keep the inferior one in line. The threat of punishment on this earth and in the hereafter was designed to create fear as a deterrent to transgression. Fear today is recognized as the greatest obstacle to fulfillment and function, to self-respect and self-realization. Far from preventing transgressions and misdeeds, fear actually promotes them. It increases rather than diminishes the probability of danger. One does not have to be afraid of automobiles in order to cross a street safely. But a person who is afraid of being hit by a car is more likely to incur such an accident. Fear is evil; it deprives us of strength, poise, clear evaluation of the situation and the determination to solve problems.

In contrast, *courage* seems to be one of the requirements of free man. The new religion will need a symbol which evokes courage, belief in one's own strength and ability. Our new concept of the universe necessitates courage. Modern man needs the courage to face uncertainties, since certainties are assured only in an autocracy. Modern man needs courage because he recognizes his own spontaneity and creativeness—and it requires courage to be spontaneous. Spontaneity is a prerequisite to self-fulfillment. It is opposed to submission, to conformity for conformity's sake. It entails the courage to be subjective with the sense of responsibility, to grant the same rights to others.

Courage is impaired by doubts in our status and worth. The assumption of our deficiency restricts our willingness and ability to co-operate and to be concerned with the welfare of others. Only a courageous person who knows his strength and has faith in himself can have faith in others; only such a person can accept the give-and-take of social living. A sense of responsibility cannot be instilled in free men by fear, but only through their feeling of belonging, their awareness of their inter-relatedness, the sureness of their own place, and their worth as persons.

VI. Mutual Aid as the New Ritual

The religious ritual will consist of mutual help. The spiritual and moral support which we all need in the discouraging tribulations in our daily lives can only come from the group where we truly are one another's brother. We need each other's help in our efforts to be as good as we

want to be, to be as effective as we can be. We need each other to remind us of our ideals and to give us the persistence to pursue them. We need each other to stimulate our devotion to the common good, to stir up our willingness, to feel with each other, to live with each other, to belong to each other.

Such a new religion will be capable of combining the collective experience of the primitive society with the individual self-realization of civilization. It will be able to use reason and present day knowledge to stir up our emotions, to bring out the best in each of us, to evoke attitudes of co-operation and courage and the resilience to resist the temptation of our own selfish interests and prejudices. It can and will provide the tools to realize the brotherhood of man. Such a religion cannot be authoritarian, only humanistic. Its faith is in man, not in God; its truth must be found through human investigation, not through revelation; its moral perspectives will be those of free men; its symbols will free man of his fears; and finally, its religious ritual will consist of mutual help so that we each can be the self-determined and self-respecting master of our fate, creator of the world around us and benefactor of this tremendous force of life around and in us.

> ❝Such a religion cannot be authoritarian, only humanistic. Its faith is in man, not in God . . . its religious ritual will consist of mutual help so that we each can be the self-determined and self-respecting master of our fate . . .❞

Exhibit 23

1956

The Sectarian Battlefront

PAUL BLANSHARD

Washington, D.C.

If federal aid for school buildings is defeated in this session of Congress, it will be the racial issue and not the religious issue that defeats it. The religious issue is scarcely being mentioned on Capitol Hill, while the racial issue, in the shape of the Powell amendment to the school-building bill, is the center of all attention. If the Powell amendment is adopted in the House and (miraculously) confirmed in the Senate in the face of a filibuster threat, those school districts which refuse to accept the Supreme Court's ruling on segregation will get no federal funds, while conforming school districts may receive substantial amounts. Will the racial rider kill the whole school-aid program?

Liberals are having a struggle of conscience and sagacity on this question. Other things being equal, they would all favor a strict ban on the payment of any money to the Southern rebels until they have accepted desegregation, but they do not want to hold up school building for years, and they fear a filibuster against any bill with a racial rider. The AFL-CIO favors bringing home the bacon for schools regardless of the evil side-effects; the NAACP and individuals like Walter Reuther favor the Powell rider.

While all eyes are focused on this racial issue, a remarkable thing has happened. The Catholic conditional boycott against federal aid to public schools has virtually faded out of the picture. The hierarchy received such feeble public support for its November demand for "welfare" funds for its school buildings that the leading Catholic legislators in Congress are not even discussing public funds for parochial schools. In the House, the two most important Catholic spokesmen on education, majority leader John McCormack and Augustine B. Kelley of Pennsylvania, sponsor of the House school-building bill, have indicated no intention of demanding federal aid for parochial schools in this session. In the Senate, three important Catholic leaders, Kennedy of Massachusetts, Murray of Montana, and McNamara of Michigan, are going along with the policy of silence.

Ten years ago this could not have happened. Then, and for many years before then, the economy-Catholic-provincial bloc stood figuratively at the door of Congress and delivered an ultimatum: Give some federal money to parochial schools for their buses, or you won't get *any* federal money for *any* regular public schools. Apparently the Catholic hierarchy realizes that it lacks the power to stop the tidal wave of sentiment for better public schools.

➤   ➤   ➤

Is humanism a religion? Most humanists would reply that if a humanist }

Paul Blanshard, a signatory of *Humanist Manifesto I*, serves as a self-proclaimed champion of the separation of church and state. As Blanshard notes, the Washington Ethical Society is a religious tax-exempt organization, as is the American Humanist Association (See Exhibits 25 and 36).

> Is humanism a religion? Most humanists would reply that if a humanist wishes to regard his personal beliefs as a religion, he is entitled to do so as much as a Methodist or a Mohammedan. Religion is neither a monopoly of theists nor an exclusive possession of the orthodox.

wishes to regard his personal beliefs as a religion, he is entitled to do so as much as a Methodist or a Mohammedan. Religion is neither a monopoly of theists not an exclusive possession of the orthodox.

But what about tax exemption for unorthodox bodies? How "religious" does an organization have to be in order to be exempted as a church under the law?

The old question has been revived in a new way here in Washington by the tax-collectors of the District of Columbia, who are trying to collect $335.60 in back taxes from the Washington Ethical Society. The Society, which has been tax exempt for eighty years, has an attractive building on Massachusetts Avenue, and a distinguished congregation of members. The Society does not endorse tax exemption for churches, but it says in effect: As long as the orthodox denominations get tax exemption, we are entitled to the same privilege.

The federal government agrees with this answer, and exempts from taxes the twenty affiliates of the American Ethical Union, but the tax collectors of the District do not accept this precedent for themselves. In a January court hearing before a Catholic judge, the Society's leader, Dr. George E. Beauchamp, answered questions from the witness stand for about three-and-one-half hours. Most of the questions were about the nature of ethical religion. The judge was obviously trying to be fair to Dr. Beauchamp, but his presuppositions were plainly drawn from the opposite end of the philosophical spectrum. Beauchamp stressed not a unity in belief but a unity in the search for truth. He emphasized the fact that religion may be a search for values with no necessary or fixed relationship to a definition of God. He pointed out that men defined God so differently that Ethical Culturists as individuals have as much claim as others to their own definitions.

Assessor James L. Martin said: "I don't care what the religion, but it must start out with belief in a supreme being." "We think, in point of fact," replied the *Washington Post*, "that by almost every objective test the society has conducted itself in the manner of a religious organization—in its regular Sunday morning meetings devoted to ethical culture, in the consecrated character of its meeting place, in the community of faith among its members. . . . It is one of the glories of the United States that the widest imaginable diversity in religious observance and belief is tolerated here."

No final decision in this case is likely before summer. Private prognostication: Even if the Society loses in the lower court, it is likely to win out before a reasonably intelligent appellate court.

➢   ➢   ➢

In New York, debate continues on the document known as the "Guide to Moral and Spiritual Values in the Schools," which the city's Board of School Superintendents proposed as a curriculum aid in reinforcing "the home and the church in strengthening belief in God." The tide is running against the proposal because the Protestant Council of the City of New York has now joined

Exhibit 24

1957

JULIAN HUXLEY

Religion without Revelation

A MENTOR BOOK
Published by THE NEW AMERICAN LIBRARY

[1957]

. . .

What, then, is religion? It is a way of life. It is a way of life which follows necessarily from a man's holding certain things in reverence, from his feeling and believing them to be sacred. And those things which are held sacred by religion primarily concern human destiny and the forces with which it comes into contact.

. . .

. . .

The idea of supernatural beings is one of the commonest among the objects, events, or ideas which are thus believed in as objects of reverence; but belief in supernatural beings is not an essential or integral part of the religious way of life, nor, conversely, are the objects of religious feeling necessarily supernatural beings.

. . .

. . .

It is often stated that the essential of religion is belief in God, meaning by that in a personal or superpersonal Divine being, or at least a belief in supernatural beings of some kind. This, however, is manifestly not true. There are whole religions which make no mention of God. The most notable example, as already mentioned, is that of Buddhism.

. . .

Thomas Henry Huxley, grandfather of Julian Huxley, helped popularize the Humanist religion by delivering evolutionary lectures that he called "lay sermons." Julian followed in his grandfather's footsteps, and was honored as the Humanist of the Year in 1962.

> ❝ [T]wentieth-century man needs a new organ for dealing with destiny, a new system of beliefs . . . in other words, a new religion. ❞

The central concept, of a process of becoming, a self-transformation of humanity with a desirable direction and rate, provides a framework of synthesis in which many conflicts can be transcended, many antithetic opposites can be reconciled—continuity and change; doubt and certainty; the immediate and the enduring; rivalry and co-operation; the actual and the possible; individualism and collectivism, at all levels from isolated individuals through family, local group, class or nation, to humanity and indeed to life as a whole.

In the actual process of individual development, the stress is seen falling on the reconciliation of conflicting impulses in a harmonious personal unity, in that of social development on the adjustment of conflicting interests in a pattern of maximum fruitfulness.

Above all, its central concept of greater fulfillment through the realisation of possibilities brings ideals and ultimate values into relation with actual imperfections and present efforts, and links them as participants in the common task of better achieving human destiny.

This brings me back to where I started—the idea of religion as an organ of destiny. It is clear, as I suggested earlier, that twentieth-century man needs a new organ for dealing with destiny, a new system of beliefs and attitudes adapted to the situation in which he and his societies now have to exist and thus an organ for the better orientation of the human species as a whole—in other words, a new religion.

Like all other new religions, and indeed all other new movements of ideas, it will at the outset be expressed and spread by a small minority: but it will in due course of time tend to become universal, not only potentially and in theory, but actually and in practice. The properties of man's psychosocial nature make this inevitable. Man cannot avoid the process of convergence which makes for the integration of divergent or hostile human groups in a single organic world society and culture.[14] And an integrated world society cannot operate effectively without an integrated common pool of thought and body of ideas. Thought and practice interact; but in the modern world thought is likely to move the faster so that a universalist system of ideas, if firmly based in reality, can be expected to play an important part in effecting the process of practical and institutional integration.

Science, as a system of discovering, organising and apply-

14   See Pere Teilhard de Chardin's remarkable book *Le Phenomene Humain* (Paris, 1955; shortly to appear in an English translation).

ing mutual knowledge, is already unified and universal in principle, though its efficiency as an organ of the human species could still be much increased. It remains for man to unify and universalise his religion.

How that religion will take form—what rituals or celebrations it might practise, whether it will equip itself with any sort of professional body or priesthood, what buildings it will erect, what symbols it will adopt—that is something which no one can prophesy. Certainly it is not a field on which the natural scientist should venture. What the scientist can do is to draw attention to the relevant facts revealed by scientific discovery, and to their implications and those of the scientific method. He can aid in the building up of a fuller and more accurate picture of reality in general and of human destiny in particular, secure in the knowledge that in so doing he is contributing to humanity's advance, and helping to make possible the emergence of a more universal and more adequate religion.

The most significant contribution of science in this vital field is the discovery of man's position and role in evolution. Let me restate this, as follows. Man is that part of reality in which and through which the cosmic process has become conscious and has begun to comprehend itself. His supreme task is to increase that conscious comprehension and to apply it as fully as possible to guide the course of events. In other words, his role is to discover his destiny as agent of the evolutionary process, in order to fulfil it more adequately. This is a practical task, to which science can and must contribute. If we want to achieve any adequate understanding and control of the electrical forces operating in nature, or the processes of plant growth and heredity, we must call on science to help. The same is true if we want to acquire any adequate understanding and control of our destiny.

Sixty-four years ago my grandfather T. H. Huxley, in his Romanes Lecture on *Evolution and Ethics*, summed up his lifelong preoccupation with the central problem of human destiny in a celebrated exhortation: 'Let us understand, once and for all, that the ethical progress of society consists not in imitating the cosmic process, still less in running away from it, but in combating it.' To-day, we must say that the ethical progress of society, and indeed human progress in all its aspects, consists not in combating the cosmic process but in wrestling with it (as Jacob wrestled with the angel), and in finding out what we can do to direct it. And this depends on our understanding of it, and on our learning how to discharge

> ❝ [I]in so doing he is contributing to humanity's advance, and helping to make possible the emergence of a more universal and more adequate religion. ❞

Exhibit 25

1959

Communist line"; Dr. Ralph Sockman, with 20; Bishop G. Bromley Oxnam, with 45; Dr. John Mackay, with 48, and Mordecai Johnson, with 16. "From the foregoing data," said the report, "it is clearly established that the leadership of the National Council of Churches, like its predecessor, the Federal Council, leans far to the left and in a large measure aids and abets the Communist conspiracy."

Shades of J. B. Matthews! The same newspapers that glorified—isn't the proper word "manufactured"?—McCarthy did not give John Bell Williams a line.

TAX-EXEMPT PACIFISM

There has been another victory for those who would interpret the word "religion" very broadly—the last two were by the Washington Ethical Society and the Fellowship of Humanity in California. This time the victor is the Fellowship of Reconciliation, which was denied tax exemption on its real estate in a New York town on the ground that pacifism is against public policy, and maybe it's illegal anyway. In the case of *Ashbrook* v. *Town of Clarkstown* the lower court ruled against the F.O.R., and the appellate court reversed by a unanimous decision. Now the F.O.R. is established as a "religious" organization, with full right to tax exemption.

MISCELLANY

• Last year it was excise tax exemption for private schools, maneuvered through Congress by that good champion of parochial schools, Aime Forand of Rhode Island. This year it is excise tax exemption for *all* private hospitals, and there is no opposition. There is nothing sectarian y'understand.

• A fairly important moral victory was scored in the House District of Columbia subcommittee when the committee voted unanimously against using government funds to subsidize streetcar fares for private-school students in Washington. The objection raised by Protestant witnesses was that this would constitute a national precedent, since Congress is a national body.

• Representative Charles E. Chamberlain, Michigan Protestant, has introduced a bill to deny the mails to (*a*) "any article, matter, thing, device, or substance of any kind which, in the opinion of the normal, reasonable, and prudent individual would appeal to prurient interest, or would suggest, induce, arouse, incite, or cause, directly or indirectly, lewd, libidinous, lustful, indecent, immoral, depraved, or obscene thoughts, desires, or acts on the part of the recipient; or (*b*) for any drug, medicine, article, or thing designed, adapted, or intended, or claimed to be so designed, adapted, or intended, for preventing conception. . . ."

Glad I am going to a nice free country like Spain.

P.B.

Page 238

THE HUMANIST
[1959, NUMBER 4]

Paul Blanshard, an editor for *The Humanist* magazine, announces that the courts have finally granted the Washington Ethical Society, the Fellowship of Humanity of California, and the Fellowship of Reconciliation tax-exempt status as "religious" organizations.

Exhibit 26

1961

488   OCTOBER TERM, 1960

                            Syllabus.   367U.S.

TORCASO *v.* WATKINS, CLERK.

APPEAL FROM THE COURT OF APPEALS OF MARYLAND

No. 373. Argued April 24, 1961.—Decided June 19, 1961.

Appellant was appointed by the Governor of Maryland to the office
of Notary Public; but he was denied a commission because he
would not declare his belief in God, as required by the Maryland
Constitution. Claiming that this requirement violated his rights
under the First and Fourteenth Amendments, he sued in a state
court to compel issuance of his commission; but relief was denied.
The State Court of Appeals affirmed, holding that the state constitutional provision is self-executing without need for implementing
legislation and requires declaration of a belief in God as a qualification for office. *Held:* This Maryland test for public office cannot
be enforced against appellant, because it unconstitutionally invades
his freedom of belief and religion guaranteed by the First Amendment and protected by the Fourteenth Amendment from infringe-
ment by the States. Pp. 489–496
223 Md. 49, 162 A. 2d 438, reversed.

Leo Pfeffer, and *Lawrence Speiser* argued the cause for
appellant. With them on the briefs were *Joseph A.
Sickles, Carlton R. Sickles, Bruce N. Goldberg, Rowland
Watts* and *George Kaufmann.*

Thomas B. Finan, Attorney General of Maryland, and *Joseph
S. Kaufman*, Deputy Attorney General, argued
the cause and filed a brief for appelle. *C. Ferdinand
Sybert*, former Attorney General of Maryland, and *Sted-
man Prescott, Jr.*, former Deputy Attorney General,
appeared with *Mr. Kaufman* on the motion to dismiss or affirm.

Briefs of *amici curiae*, urging reversal, were filed by
Herbert A. Wolff and *Leo Rosen* for the American Ethical
Union, and by *Herbert B. Ehrmann, Lawrence Peirez,
Isaac G. McNatt, Abraham Blumberg, Arnold Forster,
Paul Hartman, Theodore Leskes, Edwin J. Lukas* and *Sol
Rabkin* for the American Jewish Committee et al.

In *Torcaso v. Watkins*, a Maryland Notary Public was reinstated despite his refusal
to declare a belief in God. The Supreme Court noted that many religions, including Secular Humanism, deny the existence of God.

" Among religions in this country which do not teach what would generally be considered a belief in God are Buddhism, Taoism, Ethical Culture, Secular Humanism and others. "

TORCASO *v.* WATKINS   495

488   Opinion of the Court.

We repeat and again reaffirm that neither a State nor the Federal Government can constitutionally force a person "to profess a belief or disbelief in any religion." Neither can constitutionally pass laws or impose requirements which aid all religions as against non-believers,[10] and neither can aid those religions based on a belief in the existence of God as against those religions founded on different beliefs.[11]

In upholding the State's religious test for public office the highest court of Maryland said:

"The petitioner is not compelled to believe or disbelieve, under threat of punishment or other compulsion. True, unless he makes the declaration of belief he cannot hold public office in Maryland, but he is not compelled to hold office."

The fact, however, that a person is not compelled to hold public office cannot possibly be an excuse for barring him

---

[10] In discussing Article VI in the debate of the North Carolina Convention on the adoption of the Federal Constitution, James Iredell, later a Justice of this Court, said:

"...[I]t is objected that the people of America may, perhaps, choose representatives who have no religion at all, and that pagans and Mahometans may be admitted into offices. But how is it possible to exclude any set of men, without taking away that principle of religious freedom which we ourselves so warmly contend for?"

And another delegate pointed our that Article VI "leaves religion on the solid foundation of its own inherent validity, without any connection with temporal authority; and no kind of oppression can take place." 4 Elliot , *op. cit., supra*, at 194, 200.

[11] Among religions in this country which do not teach what would generally be considered a belief in the existence of God are Buddhism, Taoism, Ethical Culture, Secular Humanism and others. See *Washington Ethical Society v. District of Columbia*, 101 U.S. App. D. C. 371, 249 F. 2d 127; *Fellowship of Humanity v. County of Alameda*, 153 Cal. App. 2d 673, 315 P. 2d 394; II Encyclopaedia of the Social Sciences 293; 4 Encyclopaedia Britannica (1957 ed.) 325-327; 21 *id.*, at 797; Archer, Faiths Men Live By (2nd ed. revised by Purinton), 120-138, 254-313; 1961 World Almanac 695, 712; Year Book of American Churches for 1961, at 29, 47.

Exhibit 27

1968

SEEKING A FAITH FOR A NEW AGE

Essays on the Interdependence of Religion, Science and Philosophy

by
Henry Nelson Wieman

Edited and introduced by
Cedric L. Hepler

The Scarecrow Press, Inc.
Metuchen, N.J.   1975

Religion, Science and Philosophy   251

. . .

Religion, then, as the word is here used, will mean a ruling commitment practiced by a community of individuals to what they believe creates, sustains, saves, and transforms human existence toward the greatest good.

. . .

Note: The above essay was reprinted in *Seeking a Faith for a New Age* from *Zygon—Journal of Religion and Science*, March 1968, pp. 32-58.

Henry Nelson Wieman, a signatory of *Humanist Manifesto II*, provides again—as he did in his 1936 *American Philosophies of Religion*—a definition of religion that clearly encompasses Secular Humanism and other atheistic worldviews.

Exhibit 28

1973

HUMANIST MANIFESTOS I AND II

edited by Paul Kurtz

B *Prometheus Books*
700 East Amherst Street
Buffalo, New York 14215

[1973]

Preface

Humanism is a philosophical, religious, and moral point of view. . . . [The] *Humanist Manifesto I* . . . was concerned with expressing a general religious and philosophical outlook that rejected orthodox and dogmatic positions and provided meaning and direction, unity and purpose to human life. . . . What more pressing need than to recognize in this critical age of modern science and technology that, if no deity will save us, we must save ourselves. . . .

Paul Kurtz

[pages 3, 4]

From the *Humanist Manifesto II*

. . .

We find insufficient evidence for belief in the existence of a supernatural; it is either meaningless or irrelevant to the question of survival and fulfillment of the human race. . . . No deity will save us; we must save ourselves.

. . .

16

Although Paul Kurtz, author of *Humanist Manifesto II*, did not include many references to "the religion of Humanism" in the second manifesto, he nonetheless describes Humanism as "a philosophical, religious, and moral point of view." Kurtz also hints that Humanism, like every other worldview, acknowledges man's current shortcomings, offers a plan of salvation, and promises a future paradise. For the Humanist, man has problems because of an imperfect environment, he can "save" himself by restructuring society, and can thereby usher in utopia in the form of a "world community."

Exhibit 29

The Humanist Alternative:

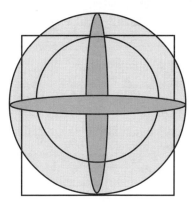

Some definitions of Humanism
Edited by Paul Kurtz

❝Humanist religion is primarily an effort to free religious faith and devotion from the dogmas of theistic theologies and supernaturalist psychologies.**❞**

II
Religious Humanism

HERBERT W. SCHNEIDER

THE TERM RELIGIOUS HUMANISM covers and confuses two quite different matters: Humanism as a religion and religion interpreted as a form of human expression and art.

Humanist religion is primarily an effort to free religious faith and devotion from the dogmas of theistic theologies and supernaturalist psychologies. Because Humanists assume (or conclude from bitter experience) that contemporary religious institutions are committed to these theologies and psychologies, they regard themselves as necessarily anti-clerical, laic or secular. As a result of their alienation from religious institutions, their conceptions of religious experience are usually individualistic and they hesitate to establish a sect or a religious organization. They may make their Humanist faith articulate by formulating a creed, but they avoid religious rites. Nevertheless, being usually on the defensive, they insist stoutly that their faith is religious and their devotion authentic even though they do not use rituals or conventional forms of worship and devoutness. They also cultivate an informal fellowship and co-operate in defence and in anti-clerical preaching. They are a militant minority whose righteous indignation and confessed reasonableness prompt them to confront organized religious bodies that cherish theistic beliefs and supernatural devotions.

Humanist interpretations of religion have a longer history and usually have operated as reform movements within particular religions, but they have become increasingly radical with the relatively recent growth of a genuine science of religion, on which Humanists depend. Humanism attempts to rid religious institutions, myths, creeds, prayers and sacraments of superstitious beliefs, while enhancing their significance as expressions of human needs, hopes and values. This goal has led Humanists into elaborate, critical analyses of religious experience, ecclesiastical forms and mythical

65

❝[Humanists] insist stoutly that their faith is religious and their devotion authentic . . .**❞**

The Humanist Alternative was published by Prometheus Books, the main Humanist publishing house. Herbert Wallace Schneider signed *Humanist Manifesto II* and has contributed essays to *Free Inquiry* magazine.

Exhibit 30

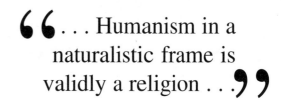

The Humanist Alternative:

" . . . Humanism in a naturalistic frame is validly a religion . . . "

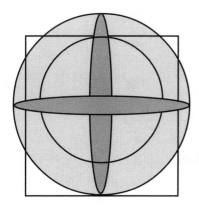

Some definitions of Humanism
Edited by Paul Kurtz

I

Humanism's Many Dimensions

EDWIN H. WILSON

THERE HAVE BEEN many Humanisms and their special emphases have each been designated by an endless array of adjectives. Christian Humanism, Greek Humanism, ethical Humanism, scientific Humanism, religious Humanism, rationalist Humanism and Humanistic Judaism are only a few of the many designations, but they are today important ones. One thing can be said, I believe, of all Humanisms that are worthy of the name: their central concern is for man, his growth, fulfillment and creativity in the here and now. Each variety of Humanism can be understood in terms of its causal sources and present programme.

The Christian Humanism that was nurtured in the Middle Ages by liberal bishops helped bring the Humanism of the Greeks down to the modern periods by means of the good libraries established by those bishops. That Christian Humanism was not anti-God but pro-man; it did not deny 'life eternal', but was concerned primarily with *this* life. Today various Christian scholars and Pope Paul are asserting that Humanism without God is futile. At the same time the liberals among the Christians are trying to recapture the word Humanism and make church ritual and actions more relevant to human need. If the action is the message—in part—there is much latent Humanism in both Jewish and Christian circles.

Religious Humanism, a term used in *A Humanist Manifesto* of 1933,[1] was based on the assumption that Humanism in a naturalistic frame is validly a religion; that all religions have been the pursuit of the ideal or the quest for the good life. The religions—natural and supernatural—are the efforts of men to be better than they are. They variously involve faith, aspiration, commitment, loyalty, hope and, sometimes, love.

[1] Sellars, Roy Wood (1933), 'A Humanist Manifesto' in *The New Humanist*, VI, 3.

15

Edwin H. Wilson, the 1979 Humanist of the Year, served as a founder and editor for *The New Humanist, The Humanist Bulletin*, and *The Humanist*, and was one of the incorporators of the American Humanist Association (AHA). In 1991 he became executive director emeritus of the AHA, as well as its official historian.

"" The popular notion that
religion is identically and
exclusively concerned
with God, immortality and
revelation is denied in the
writings of Curtis Reese,
J.A.C.F. Auer, E.S. Ames,
H.N. Wieman, Alfred
Loisy, Julian Huxley, A.E.
Haydon and many others. ""

— from page 18

Exhibit 31

GUEST EDITORIAL:
Issues That Divide: The Triumph
of Secular Humanism

LEO PFEFFER

. . .

Journal of Church and State
1977

ISSUES THAT DIVIDE: THE TRIUMPH OF SECULAR HUMANISM   211

. . .

The same development is occurring at the college level, and it is only a question of time, and a comparatively short time, before Notre Dame and Fordham will be like unto Yale and Columbia. The latter two institutions similarly started life as religious (Protestant) institutions but in time became nonsectarian, not because or at least not significantly because governmental funds would not otherwise be available to them, but simply because that is what the American college-age community wanted. In this arena, it is not Protestantism, Catholicism, or Judaism which will emerge the victor, but secular humanism, a cultural force which in many respects is stronger in the United States than any of the major religious groups or any alliance among them.

. . .

Leo Pfeffer, who victoriously argued the *Torcaso v. Watkins* case before the U.S. Supreme Court in 1961, frankly ackowledges the battle between Secular Humanism and other major religions. Pfeffer was honored as Humanist of the Year in 1988.

Exhibit 32

1983

the Humanist

JANUARY / FEBRUARY 1983 $2.50

Youth Speaks

**Winners of
the North
American
Essay Contest**

**Selected from over
300 entries**

A RELIGION FOR A NEW AGE

John J. Dunphy

[Pp. 23-26]

. . .

[T]he battle for humankind's future must be waged and won in the public school classroom by teachers who correctly perceive their role as the proselytizers of a new faith: a religion of humanity that recognizes and respects the spark of what theologians call divinity in every human being. These teachers must embody the same selfless dedication as the most rabid fundamentalist preachers, for they will be ministers of another sort, utilizing a classroom instead of a pulpit to convey humanist values in whatever subject they teach, regardless of the educational level—preschool day care or large state university. The classroom must and will become an arena of conflict between the old and the new—the rotting corpse of Christianity, together with all its adjacent evils and misery, and the new faith of humanism, resplendent in its promise of a world in which the never-realized Christian ideal of "love thy neighbor" will finally be achieved. . . . humanism will emerge triumphant. It must if the family of humankind is to survive.

P. 26

Perhaps because of his youth, John Dunphy spoke with less caution than most Humanists. His vitriolic comments about Christianity and his willingness to use the classroom to indoctrinate may shock some readers, but they pleased the editors of *The Humanist* so much that Dunphy was named one of the contest winners.

Exhibit 33

1984

It's the religion of secularism, many people don't like it,
and parents have a right to stop it!

They Are Teaching Religion in the Public Schools

RICHARD A. BAER JR.

GEORGE GALLUP has made a rather astonishing discovery, one with considerable significance for educational policy making in this country: Almost half of all Americans believe that God created man in his present form some 10,000 years.

According to a [...] port of August 29, [...] Americans polled [...] them college gra[...] Genesis account [...] rest, 38 percent b[...] man has evolved f[...] God directed that [...] cent believe in a[...] God had no part, [...] say they don't kno[...]

The reaction a[...] to the Gallup res[...] genuine surprise. [...] Bishop John S. S[...] bishop of Newark, [...] utable biblical sch[...] account of Creati[...] literally. Surprisi[...] or not, howev[...] Gallup's findin[...] shed considera[...] light on why ma[...] public school p[...] ents are speaki[...] out against the w[...] evolution is c[...] rently taught in t[...] public schools. If[...] percent of Am[...] icans believe th[...] God has guided [...] origin and devel[...] ment of huma[...] kind—and if mo[...] than half of that [...] percent reject a[...] kind of evolutiona[...] process—it is sm[...]

wonder that many object to the teaching of evolution. Especially is that true when evolution is taught as the cornerstone of a religious-philosophical world view rather than as scientific theory and the conceptual basis of modern biology.

selling book by the same title was published. The 13 hour-long TV presentations of "Cosmos" were well received by the public. The shows became required viewing for many high school biology courses across the nation, both in 1980

12

. . .

John Dewey, to take one of the most prominent and influential humanists of modern times, concluded *A Common Faith* with the following statement:

"Here are all the elements for a religious faith that shall not be confined to sect, class, or race. Such a faith has always been implicitly the common faith of mankind. It remains to make it explicit and militant."

Likewise, Corliss Lamont, who signed both the 1933 and 1973 Humanist Manifestos, argued that humanism has many similarities with religion, among which is the fact that it is "an integrated and inclusive way of life" and "a supreme commitment." Apparently thinking along the same line as Dewey and Lamont, the U.S. Supreme Court in *Torcaso* v. *Watkins* in 1961 referred to "those religions based on a belief in the existence of God as against those religions founded on different beliefs" and, in a clarifying footnote, includes "Secular Humanism" in the latter category.

The point is this: *Education never takes place in a moral and philosophical vacuum.* If the larger questions about human beings and their destiny are not being asked and answered within a predominantly Judeo-Christian framework, they will be addressed within another philosophical or religious framework—but hardly one that is "neutral." The arrogance and philosophical implausibility of secular humanism are demonstrated by the insistence of many humanists that their position possesses such neutrality, lack of dogma, and essential rationality. It is an arrogance that also quickly becomes coercive and imperialistic, as is clearly seen in the widespread opposition among such educators toward genuine choice in education, for instance, the kind of choice that would be possible through a system of education tuition vouchers.

. . .

Richard A. Baer , Jr, "They *Are* Teaching Religion in the Public Schools," *Christianity Today*, Feb. 17, 1984: 15.

Richard Baer, a Christian author, argues that Secular Humanism is religious and is taught in the public schools. This essay appeared in *Christianity Today* accompanied by several responses, both pro and con. Readers would benefit from obtaining a complete copy of the above article, including the responses.

. . .

The central point of Baer's article is right on target. The religion of secularism is being taught in our public schools. Often this is done under the guise of science, and Sagan's "Cosmos" is a notable example. In our report on the Arkansas creation-evolution trial (see *The Creator in the Courtroom*, chaps. 2 and 8 [Mott Media, 1982]), we go even further than Baer by showing how the courts have in effect established the religion of secularism in public schools. For example, the Arkansas decision (*McLean* v. *Arkansas*, 1982) disallows all views in science classes except those compatible with purely naturalistic religion, thus giving preference to these religions.

. . .

Norman Geisler in "Is Baer Right?", *Christianity Today* (February 17, 1984) p. 16.

. . .

Parents don't object to atheists and other religious humanists teaching evolution as a *theory* in our public schools. What they do object to is the teaching of *only* the theory of evolution. Why cannot *both theories* of origins be taught in a school system paid for by the taxes of the public, 82 percent of whom believe in some form of creation?

Public education today is not representative of the American people, the parents, or the taxpayers. It represents instead the secular humanist educational bureaucrats who control it and use it as a conduit to indoctrinate the minds of the youth with their religious ideology. . . .

The idea that education is neutral is a myth. Secular humanists are ardently evangelistic in their efforts to teach their values in our public schools. "Neutrality" for them means that Christians must let them, in the name of academic freedom, teach their doctrines to our children. What happened to "community public schools" that were to reflect the values of the community? They disappeared when federal aid was approved. Now only what is approved by secularists in Washington is "neutral."

. . .

Tim LaHaye in "Is Baer Right?", *Christianity Today* (February 17, 1984) p. 19.

Exhibit 34

1984

The Way of Ethical Humanism

by Gerald A. Larue

A Religion to Meet the Psychological Needs of Our Time.

"A Religion to Meet the Psychological Needs of Our Time"

. . .

Humanism is a way of life that involves joyous service for the greater good of humanity in this one and only life. We believe that in human beings there is that which is worthy of ethical or religious commitment. . . . Our humanist faith can be justified only by the quality of human relationships resulting from our attempt to live the humanist way of life.

Unlike other religions . . . in humanism there is no supernaturalistic, paternalistic deity who has revealed his will for humans and who has made clear that there are punishments for disobedience to that will and rewards for obedience. We have no revealer of ultimate truth. . . .

We have no belief in an afterlife. . . . There are no sacred scriptures, no salvation. . . .

20   THE HUMANIST

. . .

Our religion is based upon the best that we know about our cosmos, our world, and ourselves. . . . We recognize our oneness with the cosmos and our spatial and temporal minuteness. We see the human as the end-product of more than 17 billion years of evolution of the cosmos, the 4.5 billion years of evolution of our solar system and our earth. We see ourselves as the highest life-form the evolutionary process has developed, unique on our planet, and perhaps unique within the entire cosmos, for at this moment we have no knowledge of any other intelligent beings in the cosmos. As a species we are therefore precious.

. . .

SEPTEMBER/OCTOBER 1984   21

Gerald A. Larue, a signatory of *Humanist Manifesto II*, was the 1989 Humanist of the Year. As a Senior Editor of the Humanist magazine *Free Inquiry*, Larue acknowledges Humanism as "a religion."

94

Exhibit 35

1985

Auburn University

DIRECTORY 1985/86
STUDENT/FACULTY

" AUBURN PASTORS
AND
CAMPUS MINISTERS
. . .
HUMANIST
Humanist Counselor
Delos McKown "

AUBURN PASTORS AND CAMPUS MINISTERS

ASSEMBLY OF GOD
Auburn Assembly of God 555-1692
   North College Street at Drake Avenue
   Rudet Adkinson, Pastor (home: 555-7477)

AUBURN CHRISTIAN FELLOWSHIP
110 Miller Ave. 555-3963
Dean Collins, Campus Minister 555-6983

BAPTIST
Baptist Student Union 555-6521
   135 North College Street
   Clete Sipes, Campus Minister
   (home: 555 -7670)
   Ben Hale,
      Assoc. Campus Minister 555-8616

Ebenezer Baptist Church 555-2919
   54 Pitts Street
   Willie Muse, Pastor
   (home: 555-2151 Montgomery)

Farmville Baptist Church 555-7361
   Highway 147 (North College Street Extension)
   J. C. Farrington, Pastor (home: 555-7361)

First Baptist Church 555-8506
   East Glenn Avenue at North College Street
   John H. Jeffers, Pastor (home: 555-5903)

CATHOLIC
Catholic Student Center 555-5540
   234 East Magnolia Ave.
   Sister Sharon Haskins (home: 555-0588)

CHARISMATIC FELLOWSHIP
Word of Life
   World Outreach Center 555-9959
   1415 Moores Mill Rd.
   Dave Fisher (home: 555-6042)

CHRISTIAN (Disciples of Christ)
Village Christian Church 555-5111
   141 Cox Street

CHRISTIAN SCIENCE
Christian Science College
   Organization 555-5434
   Mrs. Irene Gill, Adviser (home: 555-5434)
Christian Science Society 555-3079
   134 Cary Drive

CHURCH OF JESUS CHRIST OF LATTER DAY SAINTS
Auburn Branch 555-6485
   2324 Loachapoka Hwy (14)

EPISCOPAL
Chapel of St. Dunstan of Canterbury and the
Episcopal College Center 555-5657
   136 East Magnolia Avenue
   John R. Gilchrist, Chaplain (home: 555-1359)

HUMANIST
Humanist Counselor 555-8710
   Delos McKown (home: 555-8710)

JEWISH
B'nai B'rith Hillel 555-9550
   442 Cary Drive
   Dr. and Mrs. Leo J. Hirth, Counselors
   (home: 555-9550)

LUTHERAN
Lutheran Student Fellowship 555-3901
   446 South Gay Street
Trinity Lutheran Church 555-3901
   446 South Gay Street
   Ron Biel, Minister (home: 555-7441)

METHODIST
AME Zion 555-1802
   221 Donahue Drive

Auburn United Methodist
   Church 555-8800
   220 East Magnolia Avenue

Auburn University treats Humanism as a religion. During the day, Dr. Delos B. McKown teaches philosophy at Auburn; at night he serves as a Humanist counselor. McKown is a contributing editor for *Free Inquiry* magazine, and, according to the *Wall Street Journal*, recently protested efforts to include *Of Pandas and People* by Percival Davis and Dean Kenyon in the public schools. The reason? McKown complained that the concept of a designer violated the separation of church and state!

Exhibit 36

1986

Free Inquiry

Winter 1986/87   Vol. 7, No. 1 $3.75

The New
Inquisition
in the Schools

God and Morality
Sidney Hook

Naturalistic
Humanism
Corliss Lamont

st Sexual Morality
ncoeur

'undamentalism
wide

ment Was Written
Larue

manist Center; More on
h-Healing; Atheism in the Soviet
ion; Humanism in Mexico and
e Mormon Church

· · ·

But is secular humanism a religion? The lawyers in this case insist that it is and they subpoenaed the bylaws and other documents of the major U.S. humanist organizations to prove it. The organized humanist movement in America is put in a quandary; for the Fellowship of Religious Humanists (300 members), the American Ethical Union (3,000 members), and the Society for Humanistic Judaism (4,000 members) consider themselves to be religious. Even the American Humanist Association (3,500 members), which has both religious and nonreligious members and is often considered to be a "naturalistic humanist" association, has a *religious* tax exemption. (I should point out that I and others have repeatedly urged the AHA to abandon its religious exemption, but to no avail.) Regrettably there are no humanist membership organizations that are nonreligious in legal status. The *only* exception is the Council for Democratic and Secular Humanism (publisher of FREE INQUIRY magazine), which has a nonprofit *educational* exemption, but as yet has not been a membership organization.

· · ·

Winter 1986/87   5

Free Inquiry, a prominent Humanist publication, is edited by Dr. Paul Kurtz. In the above excerpt, Kurtz admits that all formal Humanist membership organizations in America either consider themselves explicitly religious, or claim 501(c)3 religious tax exempt status.

❝Even the American Humanist Association (3,500 members) . . . has a *religious* tax exemption.**❞**

Exhibit 37

1986

CENSORSHIP
EVIDENCE OF BIAS
IN OUR CHILDREN'S
TEXTBOOKS

Paul C. Vitz

SERVANT BOOKS
Ann Arbor, Michigan
1986

❝[A] very widespread secular and liberal mindset . . . pervades the leadership in the world of education (and textbook publishing) and a secular and liberal bias is its inevitable consequence.❞

ONE

Censorship in Public School Textbooks: An Overview

THE STUDY DESCRIBED HERE was conducted to answer some important and basic questions. Are public school textbooks biased? Are they censored? The answer to both is yes. And the nature of the bias is clear: Religion, traditional family values, and conservative political and economic positions have been reliably excluded from children's textbooks. This exclusion is particularly disturbing because it is found in a system paid for by taxpayers, and one that claims, moreover, to be committed to impartial knowledge and accuracy.

In spite of the biases such as those that are described here there is no evidence of any kind of conscious conspiracy operating to censor textbooks. Instead, a very widespread secular and liberal mindset appears to be responsible. This mindset pervades the leadership in the world of education (and textbook publishing) and a secular and liberal bias is its inevitable consequence.

In the first part of this project a total of sixty representative social studies textbooks were carefully evaluated. In grades 1 through 4 these books introduce the child to U.S. society—to family life, community activities, ordinary economic transactions, and some history. None of the books covering grades 1 through 4 contain one word referring to any religious activity in contemporary American life. For example, not one word refers to

1

This study on censorship of children's textbooks by Paul C. Vitz was funded by the federal government's National Institute of Education (NIE), part of the Department of Education. Vitz's conclusion: These textbooks are heavily biased in favor of the Secular Humanist worldview and against the Christian worldview. We also recommend Phylis Schlafly's *Child Abuse in the Classroom*.

66 Most disturbing was the constant omission of reference to the large role that religion has always played in American life. This fact has been seen as a fundamental feature of American society by foreign observers since de Tocqueville. 99

any child or adult who prayed, or who went to church or temple. The same was true for the twenty grade 5 and 6 texts, as well. An occasional rare picture (without captions) in these sixty books does depict Jewish, Catholic, Amish, or vague nondenominational religious scenes. The few pictures, all told there were only eleven, that do refer to religious activity were distributed over sixty books and roughly 15,000 pages. In any case, not one word or image in any book shows any form of contemporary representative Protestantism.

In a very general way the family is often mentioned in the textbooks, but the idea that marriage is the origin and foundation of the family is never presented. Indeed, the words *marriage*, *wedding*, *husband*, *wife*, do not occur once in these books. Nowhere is it suggested that being a mother or homemaker was a worthy and important role for a woman.

The fifth grade U.S. history texts include modest coverage of religion in colonial America and in the early Southwest missions; however, the treatment of the past 100 or 200 years is so devoid of reference to religion as to give the impression that it has almost ceased to exist in America. The sixth grade books deal with world history or world culture, and they neglect, often to the point of serious distortion, Jewish and Christian historical contributions.

Social studies books frequently select individuals to serve as "role models," that is, to represent important, admirable Americans. Such figures are given a photo and special coverage of their lives. For grades 1 through 6, a total of twenty-three role models who had political or ideological significance for U.S. society since World War II were identified. Typical selections include Eleanor Roosevelt, Martin Luther King, Jr., Margaret Mead, Rachel Carson, and Los Angeles Mayor Tom Bradley. Only one of the role models (Clare Booth Luce) is a conservative. Most of the role models are Democrats and the few Republicans (former Rep. Millicent Fenwick and Sen. Nancy Kassebaum) are women. Not one contemporary role model is conservative and male, and no person from business since World War II was selected.

High school books covering U.S. history were also studied, and none came close to adequately presenting the major religious events of the past 100 to 200 years. Most disturbing was the }

{ constant omission of reference to the large role that religion has always played in American life. This fact has been seen as a fundamental feature of American society by foreign observers since de Tocqueville.

A total of 670 stories and articles from grades 3 and 6 were also analyzed. A very small number of stories have religion as a secondary theme, but no story featured Christian or Jewish religious motivation, although one story does make American Indian religion the central theme in the life of an American white girl. Again, there was not one reference to Protestant religious life.

Another notable finding is that business was ignored. No Horatio Alger stories appear in these readers. No story features an immigrant who makes good in America in business or in a profession. Almost no story featured marriage or motherhood as important or positive, nor does any story give any positive significance to babies. But there are many aggressively feminist stories that openly deride traditional manhood.

Some particular examples of the bias against religion are significant. One social studies book has thirty pages on the Pilgrims, including the first Thanksgiving. But there is not one word (or image) that referred to religion as even a part of the Pilgrims' life. One mother whose son is in a class using this book wrote me to say that he came home and told her that "Thanksgiving was when the Pilgrims gave thanks to the Indians." The mother called the principal of this suburban New York City school to point out that Thanksgiving was when the Pilgrims thanked God. The principal responded by saying "that was her opinion"—the schools could only teach what was in the books!

Another social studies text has a page on Joan of Arc in which there was no reference to *any* religious aspect of her life. This is an obvious serious misrepresentation of her historical meaning. (Apparently Joan of Arc was included because she was a woman of historical importance.)

Another example is provided by a story of the Nobel laureate and Jewish writer Isaac Bashevis Singer. In his original story the main character, a boy, prayed "to God" and later remarked "Thank God." In the story presented in the sixth grade reader the words "to God" were taken out and the expression "Thank

66 One social studies book has thirty pages on the Pilgrims, including the first Thanksgiving. But there is not one word (or image) that referred to religion as even a part of the Pilgrims' life. One mother whose son is in a class using this book wrote me to say that he came home and told her that "Thanksgiving was when the Pilgrims gave thanks to the Indians." 99

God" was changed to "Thank goodness." These changes not only represent a clear case of removing God from our textbooks, but they also transform the story. That is, by removing God, the spiritual dimension is taken out, and the story's clear answer to the boy's prayer is blunted or negated; and, of course, the historical accuracy of the author's portrayal of small town Jewish life in Eastern Europe is also falsified.

Many other examples of bias like those just mentioned are also described in the next four chapters.

I assume the reader already acknowledges that the content of school textbooks is important. The facts, interpretations, and values taught today's children will largely determine the character of tomorrow's citizenry. Indeed, it has been said that to control the content of a nation's textbooks is to control that nation's future. This, of course, is too extreme a statement since children learn much from sources other than textbooks. Nevertheless, C.S. Lewis was certainly right when he wrote, as the first sentence of his *Abolition of Man*, "I doubt whether we are sufficiently attentive to the importance of elementary textbooks." I know I was not sufficiently attentive until this project forced me to take a careful look. What I saw has certainly roused me from my educational slumber. It may do the same for you.

❝The facts, interpretations, and values taught today's children will largely determine the character of tomorrow's citizenry. Indeed, it has been said that to control the content of a nation's textbooks is to control that nation's future. This, of course, is too extreme a statement since children learn much from sources other than textbooks.❞

❝Whether one calls it secular humanism, enlightenment universalism, skeptical modernism, or just plain permissive liberalism, the bottom line is that a very particular and narrow sectarian philosophy has taken control of American education.❞

school administrators have suffered. Such a system could not reform itself even if it wanted to for the simple reason that it doesn't control itself. The schools are no longer autonomous, even with respect to the basic issues of discipline or curriculum content.

3. *The antitraditional values of the education leadership.* A major reason for not expecting change is that many leaders of the public schools seem to be personally opposed to traditional values and seem much less religious than the public at large. For years the philosophy of education dominating the country's schools of education has been uniformly liberal, secular, and even anti-religious. This should not be surprising; years ago, John Dewey's philosophy came to dominate American education, most especially our schools of education. From these schools, his ideas spread to principals and teachers until now Dewey's position is ubiquitous. And Dewey himself was strongly hostile to traditional religion with its belief in a transcendent reality and in revelation. For Dewey of course, traditional religion primarily meant Christianity. Dewey was an acknowledged leader in what has since been called secular humanism, a movement officially launched with a *Humanist Manifesto* in 1933, a manifesto that was largely the consequence of Dewey's energy and prestige.[19]

Since then, countless other secularists have furthered the movement to control educational philosophy and practice. Examples of important psychologists with major impact on the schools of education are Carl Rogers and B.F Skinner—both well known humanists hostile to traditional religion.[20] Their impact on counseling and learning theories has been nothing less than immense. The secularization of moral education is best shown by Lawrence Kohlberg[21] and the values clarification theorists Raths and Simon.[22] All of these academics are well known humanists. Whether one calls it secular humanism, enlightenment universalism, skeptical modernism, or just plain permissive liberalism, the bottom line is that a very particular and narrow sectarian philosophy has taken control of American education. This philosophy is one that occupies a small part of the American ideological and political spectrum. Besides excluding most of the usual conservative viewpoints, it rejects much of

❝Given the overwhelming secular philosophies characterizing American education in the last fifty years, it is to be expected that leaders in education will differ markedly from the general American public in the area of basic moral values.❞

libertarianism; it also rejects some of the still more radical positions on the left.

Given the overwhelming secular philosophies characterizing American education in the last fifty years, it is to be expected that leaders in education will differ markedly from the general American public in the area of basic moral values. This has been documented in the *Connecticut Mutual Life Report on American Values in the 80s*,[23] where, for example, it is reported that 65% of the general public describe it as wrong; 74% of our education leaders say that abortion is "not a moral issue."[24] Likewise on many other traditional values and moral issues, the education leaders are reported to be markedly more liberal than the public. Education leaders, for example, overwhelmingly say homosexuality and lesbianism are not morally wrong.[25] This report documents the case that the leaders of education are consistently more liberal than leaders of business, voluntary associations, the military, and not surprisingly, religious leaders. It is interesting to note that government leaders had moral positions very similar to those in education.[26]

A recent Gallup Poll shows that 95% of the American public reports a belief in God (a figure that has remained unchanged since 1944 when Gallup first asked the question.) In a typical month, over 50% of American go to a religious service. But one would not know this from reading our school textbooks. Any approach to education that omits reference to something that is believed in by 95% of the country is very rightly called narrow and sectarian.

There are, of course, many individual teachers who do hold traditional values, conservative economic and political views, and who are religious. But they are hard put to affect education policy because their leaders, as noted above, usually hold different views than they do. In general, the typical teacher does represent typical American values—but the curriculum is primarily controlled by those at the top, and they show little regard for the mores and values of the typical teacher or parent.

Some teachers, of course, still introduce God, prayer, and traditional concepts of right and wrong into their teaching or

❝There are, of course, many individual teachers who do hold traditional values, conservative economic and political views, and who are religious. But they are hard put to affect education policy because their leaders, as noted above, usually hold different views than they do. In general, the typical teacher does represent typical American values—but the curriculum is primarily controlled by those at the top, and they show little regard for the mores and values of the typical teacher or parent.❞

Exhibit 38

1987

American Education on Trial

Is Secular Humanism a Religion?

The Opinion of
Judge W. Brevard Hand
in the Alabama Textbook Case

With an Introduction
by
Richard John Neuhaus

CENTER FOR JUDICIAL STUDIES

Americans was found to be religious. However, the non-religious character of a movement, as demonstrated by the adherents' behavior, will undercut protestations of sincerity. *See, e.g., United States v. Kuch*, 299 F. Sup. 439 (D. D.C. 1968), in which drug use was not rendered religious by a camouflage of ritual. By the same logic, an allegedly non-religious movement may be shown by the adherent's behaviour to actually be religious. *See, e.g., Malnak v. Yogi*, 592 F.2d 197 (3d Cir. 1979) in which the Science of Creative Intelligence—Transcendental Meditation was held religious, not scientific. Sincerity is an important factor because the courts are accustomed to deciding questions of credibility and veracity, while the state is incompetent to issue decrees on the validity of belief.[43]

Another factor is group organization and hierarchical structure,[44] which evidence the social characteristics of a movement, and show that the adherents sincerely follow a theory of human relationship.[45] Literary manifestations of a movement may also be important, particularly if they take the form of an authoritative text.[46] Ritual and worship also would be significant because they would be evidence of the religion's belief about supernatural or transcendent reality.

Humanism A Religion?

In the present case, the plaintiffs contend that a particular belief system fits within the first amendment definition of religion. The plaintiffs' experts used several different labels in referring to this belief system. Dr. Timothy Smith used the phrase "atheistic humanism." Trans. at 113. Dr. James Davison Hunter used "naturalistic humanism." Dr. William R. Coulson accepted these terms, as well as "religious humanism," a term John Dewey used. Trans. at 498, 507. Dr. James Hitchcock used nontheistic humanism as a synonym for humanism, Trans. at 741-42, and secular humanism as encompassing atheistic and nontheistic humanism. Trans. at 742. Dr. Richard A Baer, Jr. used "humanism" to refer to secular humanism and atheistic humanism. Trans. at 812.[47] All of the experts, and the class representatives,[48] agreed that this belief system is a religion which:

makes a statement about supernatural existence
a central pillar of its logic;
defines the nature of man;
sets forth a goal or purpose for individual
and collective human existence; and

[43]*Id.* at 836. *See also Riga, Religion, Sincerity and Free Exercise,* 25 *Cath. Law.* 246, 160-61 (1980).
[44]Testimony of Dr. James Davison Hunter, Trans. at 263; Testimony of Dr. James Hitchcock, Trans. at 748-49, 768-69.
[45]Dr. Hunter concentrated on the sociological aspects of religion. His testimony referred to numerous social manifestations of religion might exhibit. *See Dodge, The Free Exercise of Religion: A Sociological Approach,* 67 *Mich. L. R.* 679 (1969) for one commentator's notion that a religion should be defined purely by functional criteria. The analysis is, however, inadequate, and would include many non-religious activities.
[46]Testimony of Dr. Hunter, Trans. at 263-64; Testimony of Dr. Hitchcock, Trans. 748, 769-70.
[47]Much, if not all, of the variety in language denominating the belief system under consideration arose from the differing disciplines from which the experts approached the topic, and the fact that a number of witnesses believed that other labels, while essentially correct, had been overused by the public and popular press and turned into mere epithets.
[48]Whorton, Trans. at 389; Webster, Trans. at 424-25; Smith, Trans. at 452-53.

46

As one might expect, the mass of evidence demonstrating that Secular Humanism is a religion has prompted some parents and teachers to challenge Humanism's monopoly in the public schools. One such challenge was issued in Alabama, where parents brought action against a Mobile school board and the governor for "establishing" the religion of Humanism in the classroom. The Chief Judge of a U.S. District Court in Alabama, William Brevard Hand, agreed with the parents' conclusions. Unfortunately, his decision was later overturned.

defines the nature of the universe, and
thereby delimits its purpose

It purports to establish a closed definition of reality; not closed in that adherents know everything, but in that every thing is knowable: can be recognized by the human intellect aided only by the devices of that intellect's own creation or discovery. The most important belief of this religion is its denial of the transcendent and/or supernatural: there is no God, no creator, no divinity. By force of logic the universe is thus self-existing, completely physical and hence, essentially knowable. Man is the product of evolutionary, physical, forces. He is purely biological and has no supernatural or transcendent spiritual component or quality. Man's individual purpose is to seek and obtain personal fulfillment by freely developing every talent and ability, especially his rational intellect, to the highest level.[49] Man's collective purpose is to seek the good life by the increase of every person's freedom and potential for personal development.[50]

In addition, humanism, as a belief system, erects a moral code and identifies the source of morality. This source is claimed to exist in humans and the social relationships of humans. Again, there is no spiritual or supernatural origin for morals: man is merely physical, and morals, the rules governing his private and social conduct, are founded only on man's actions, situation and environment. In addition to a moral code, certain attitudes and conduct are proscribed since they interfere with personal freedom and fulfillment. In particular any belief in a deity or adherence to a religious system that is theistic in any way is discouraged.

Secular humanism, or humanism in the sense of a religious belief system, (as opposed to humanism as just an interest in the humanities), has organizational characteristics. Some groups are more structured and hierarchical, others less so. These include the American Humanist Association, the Council for Democratic and Secular Humanism, and the Fellowship of Religious Humanists.[51] These organizations proselytize and preach their theories with the avowed purpose of persuading non-adherents to believe as they do. They conduct seminars and retreats, with various organizations cooperating in such activities.

These organizations publish magazines, newsletters and other periodicals, including *Free Inquiry, The Humanist* and *Progressive World.*[52] The entire body of thought has three key documents that furnish the text upon which the belief system rests as on a platform: *Humanist Manifesto I, Humanist Manifesto II,* and the *Secular Humanist Declaration.*

These factors noted in the two preceding paragraphs demonstrate the *institutional* character of secular humanism. They are evidence that this belief system is similar to groups traditionally afforded protection by the first amendment religion clauses.

---

[49]Testimony of Dr. Paul Kurtz, Trans. at 1687-88, 1697-98. The tenets of this belief-system are succinctly expressed in *Humanist manifesto I* and *Humanist Manifesto II.*

[50]*See, e.g.,* Kurtz, *Preface to Humanist Manifestos I and II* at 3 (1978) ("If the starting point of humanism is the preservation and enhancement of all things human, then what more worthwhile goal than the realization of the human potentiality of each individual and of humanity as a whole?") *See also Humanist Manifesto I, Id.* at 10 "[T]he quest for the good life is still the central task for mankind."

[51]Dr. Hunter, Trans. at 262-63.

[52]*Id.* at 264.

Furthermore, the movement has leaders, alive and deceased, who are acknowledged, even revered, as authorities on its purposes and application in daily life. These include John Dewey, Sidney Hook, Paul Kurtz and Corliss Lamont.[53] These men do not present a monolithic front,[54] and this is another factor evidencing this as a religious movement. There is a diversity of views and philosophies within the humanist community very similar to the schisms and debates existing within the Christian, Jewish and Muslim communities.[55]

Dr. Paul Kurtz testifies that secular humanism is a scientific methodology, not a religious movement. In his testimony he attempted to make a case that humanism generally, and secular humanism in particular, is the entire body of western philosophical and scientific thought. He thus attempted to claim for this ideology the heritage of learning found in all prior western civilizations. Dr. Kurtz's attempt to revise history to comply with his personal beliefs is of no concern to this Court. Whether his concept of history and western civilization is true is irrelevant. It may be that Dr. Kurtz really does perceive himself as one of a group of scholars committed to the continuation of this tradition. For first amendment purposes, the commitment of humanists to a non-supernatural and non-transcendent analysis, even to the point of hostility towards and outright attacks on all theistic religions, prevents them from maintaining the fiction that this is a non-religious discipline. This Court is concerned with the logic and consistency, the rationality, one might say, of Dr. Kurtz's contention that secular humanism is not a religious system, but science. Secular humanism is religious for first amendment purposes because it makes statements based on faith-assumptions.

To say that science is only concerned with data collected by the five senses as enhanced by technological devices of man's creation is to define *science's* limits. These are the parameters within which scientists function. However, to claim that there is nothing real beyond observable data is to make an assumption based not on science, but on faith, faith that observable data is all that is real. A statement that there is no transcendent or supernatural reality is a religious statement. A statement that there is no scientific proof of supernatural or transcendent reality is irrelevant and nonsensical, because inquiry into the fundamental nature of man and reality itself may not be confined solely within the sphere of physical, tangible, observable science.[56]

To demand that there be physical proof of the supernatural, and to claim that an apparent lack of proof means the supernatural cannot be accepted, is to create a religious creed. It is not scientific to say that because there is no physical proof of the supernatural, we must base moral theories on disbelief and skepticism.[57] If there is no evidence, the theory, one way or the other, has nothing to do with

---

[53]Testimony of Mr. Paul Kurtz, Trans. at 1698-1700.

[54]*Id.*

[55]Dr. Baer, Trans. at 855-56.

[56]The fact that such inquiry can be, and often is, conducted by systematic and quantifiable methods does not make the inquiry itself one belonging to the physical sciences.

[57]In particular, morals are inevitably based on theories of man's nature and ideas about his purpose and destiny. As science does not inquire whether man has a supernatural nature or not, the foundation for a moral theory cannot be represented as having a scientific basis. Therefore, it is specious and false to represent as a scientific and non-religious statement the claim that "morals must not be based on supernatural beliefs."

48

science. Religious persons can and do conduct rational and systematic debate on matters of faith. The physical sciences do not preclude religious faith. They examine other areas of inquiry, and are unconcerned, yet compatible with, religious inquiry.[58] The Court is holding that the promotion and advancement of a religious system occurs when one faith-theory is taught to the exclusion of others and this is prohibited by the first amendment religion clauses.

Dr. Kurtz's testimony that secular humanism has no religious aspect is not logical. For purposes of the first amendment, secular humanism is a religious belief system, entitled to the protections of, and subject to the prohibitions of, the religion clauses. It is not mere scientific methodology that may be promoted and advanced in the public schools.

Religious Promotion in Textbooks?

The Court now considers whether this religious belief system of Humanism (in whatever particular strain it occurs) is involved in a constitutional controversy before this Court. As already noted,[59] the Supreme Court has declared that teaching religious tenets in such a way as to promote or encourage a religion violates the religion clauses. This prohibition is not implicated by mere coincidence of ideas with religious tenets.[60] Rather, there must be systematic, whether explicit or implicit, promotion of a belief system as a whole. The facts showed that the State of Alabama has on its state textbook list certain volumes that are being used by school systems in this state, which engage in such promotion.

The parties presented various experts who examined different types of texts. Dr. Timothy Smith and Dr. Paul Vitz conducted examinations of high school history texts.[61] Dr. Vitz analyzed all of the listed social studies books, and Dr. Hunter analyzed all non-fifth grade social studies books. The home economics books were reviewed by Dr. Coulson, Dr. Baer, Dr. Strike, Dr. Spykman, Dr. Kurtz, and Dr. Halpin. Additionally, Verdene Ryder, the author of *Contemporary Living*, Robert F. Baker and Dr. Charles Rudder testified about the quality of school textbooks in general.

The virtually unanimous conclusion of the numerous witnesses, both expert and lay, party and non-party, was that textbooks in the fields examined were poor from an educational perspective. Mere rotten and inadequate textbooks,

---

[58]Dr. Charles Rudder, a witness proffered by the State Board of Education testified that it was not rationally possible to "defend the claim that on the basis of what we know about the natural, we know anything about the supernatural or can draw any conclusions one way or another about the supernatural. It would appear to me that if the supernatural exists, we can be informed about the natural from the supernatural, but we can't inform ourselves about the supernatural from the natural." Tr. at 2122.

[59]*See*, Discussion, supra, at 86.

[60]See, e.g., *McGowan, Supra*, note 34. As previously observed, plaintiffs do not contend that mere exposure to ideas and concepts of humanism violates their rights.

[61]Dr. Smith studied all ten listed books, plus two other eleventh grade texts that were not introduced: *America! America!*, see page 97; *A People and a Nation*, State List, p. 97. He also analyzed an eighth grade book: *We The People*, State List, p. 92. The complete list of books examined by Dr. Smith is Plaintiffs' Exhibit 174. Dr. Paul Vitz examined all of the history texts listed in the body of the opinion, supra, except for *Our American Heritage*, Exhibit 53, and *A History of the United States*, defendant-intervenors' Exhibit 6. The list of books reviewed by Dr. Vitz is plaintiffs' Exhibit 16A.

49

Exhibit 39

1988

*the*Humanist

SEPTEMBER/OCTOBER 1988 $3.00

Faith Healing

Behind the Drama of the Gods

How Religious Is Secular Humanism?

A single footnote to the landmark Torcaso case is creating more confusion and ambiguity than it ever could have eliminated

by Leo Pfeffer

[Pp.13-18, 50]

Fundamentalists, individually or collectively, have manifested no indication of giving up in their crusade against secular humanism in the public schools. If the Supreme Court upholds one book, the fundamentalists will find another one to attack, and to this there will be no end until the Supreme Court rules clearly and definitely that footnote eleven in *Torcaso*, as far as it relates to secular humanism, was erroneous and not to be followed. Should, on the other hand, the Court accept the validity of the fundamentalists' claim, the consequence may be no less than the disintegration of our public school system and the end of Horace Mann's dream.

THE HUMANIST   50

Ironically, Leo Pfeffer's 1961 *Torcaso v. Watkins* victory in the U.S. Supreme Court created a dilemma for the Secular Humanist movement. In a footnote, the Court acknowledged Secular Humanism as a religion, which would seem to indicate that Humanism in the public schools represents a violation of church and state. Pfeffer now recognizes the threat posed by the footnote.

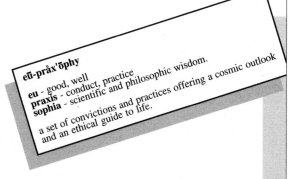

Exhibit 40

1989

EUPRAXOPHY
LIVING WITHOUT RELIGION

eū-prăx'ōphy
eu - good, well
praxis - conduct, practice
sophia - scientific and philosophic wisdom.

a set of convictions and practices offering a cosmic outlook
and an ethical guide to life.

PAUL KURTZ

PROMETHEUS BOOKS
700 EAST AMHERST STREET - BUFFALO, NEW YORK 14215

[1989]

EUPRAXOPHY DEFINED
...

In making the distinction between a nonreligious, secular humanism and religious humanism, I surely do not wish to fracture the humanist movement. But there already exists a deep division on this point. Many religious humanists continue to insist not only that they are religious but that secular humanism is a religion. They especially look to humanistic Unitarian churches, Ethical Culture societies, or Humanistic Judaism temples as their models. Most Unitarian churches or societies are not humanist, but are vaguely Christian, or theistic, even though a significant number of Unitarians identify with humanism. Even in humanist churches, societies, and temples, there is a minister or leader who tends his congregation, delivers sermons on Sundays, and administers pastoral counseling—as do his theistic counterparts. Granted that the religious humanist is a nontheist who rejects the existence of God; yet in adopting the term *religious*, he only obfuscates the true character of humanism as a radical alternative to theism.

EUPRAXOPHY DEFINED

If humanism is not a religion, what is it? Unfortunately, there is no word in the English language adequate to describe it fully—though there are words in other languages that do. Humanism combines, as I will argue, a method of inquiry, a cosmic world view, a life stance, and a set of social values. The Dutch, for example, have the word *levensbeschouwing*, which can be translated as "reflection on, consideration of, or view of life." Dutch also has the adjective *levensovertuiging*, which is stronger than *levensbeschouwing* because *overtuiging* means "conviction." Thus there are no religious overtones. *Religion* in Dutch is *godsdienst*, which means "service to God." English has no such terminology.

...

13

Paul Kurtz, author of *Humanist Manifesto II*, editor of *Free Inquiry*, and publisher of Prometheus Books, attempts in this book to prove that Secular Humanism is not a religion. In the process, Kurtz has to invent new terms to describe Secular Humanism. Kurtz understands that almost everyone cited in these exhibits believes that Humanism is a religion, and that atheistic faiths are functionally religious. But he knows that if Secular Humanism is a religion, then it should not be allowed in the public schools, according to the current interpretation of the First Amendment.

> **❝[E]upraxophy . . . provides a coherent, ethical life stance . . . it presents a cosmic theory of reality. . . defends a set of criteria governing the testing of truth claims . . . advocates an ethical posture. And it is committed implicitly or explicitly to a set of political ideals. Eupraxophy combines both a *Weltanshauung* and a philosophy of living.❞**

EUPRAXOPHY DEFINED
...

Eupraxophy differs from antiseptically neutral philosophy in that it enters consciously and forthrightly into the marketplace where ideas contend. Unlike pure philosophy, it is not simply the *love* of wisdom, though this is surely implied by it, but also the *practice* of wisdom. By that I do not mean that ethicists should not be interested in developing the capacity for critical ethical judgment or practical wisdom. That is an eminent goal. But eupraxophy goes further than that, for it provides a coherent, ethical life stance. Moreover, it presents a cosmic theory of reality that seems reasonable at a particular point in history in the light of the best knowledge of the day. Humanist eupraxophy defends a set of criteria governing the testing of truth claims. It also advocates an ethical posture. And it is committed implicitly or explicitly to a set of political ideals. Eupraxophy combines both a *Weltanshauung* and a philosophy of living. But it takes us one step further by means of commitment; based upon cognition, it is fused with passion. It involves the application of wisdom to the conduct of life.

17

EUPRAXOPHY DEFINED
...

Humanist eupraxophy, on the other hand, attempts to draw the philosophical implication of science to the life of man. It seeks to develop a cosmic perspective, based on the most reliable findings encountered on the frontiers of science. It recognizes the gaps in knowledge and the things we do not know that still need to be investigated. It is keenly aware of the need for fallibilism and agnosticism about what we do and do not know. Yet it boldly applies practical scientific wisdom to life.

Eupraxophy, unlike philosophy or science, does not focus on one specialized field of knowledge; it seeks to understand the total impact of scientific knowledge on a person's life. Yet the areas of philosophy, science, and eupraxophy are not rigid. Philosophers can assist scientists in interpreting their discoveries and relating them to other fields of inquiry, and in developing a broader point of view. Still, eupraxophy moves beyond philosophy and science in seeking to present a coherent life view as the basis on which we are willing to act. It is the ground upon which we stand, the ultimate outlook that controls our view of reality.

Accordingly, the primary task of eupraxophy is to understand nature and life and to draw concrete normative prescriptions from

19

THE DEFINITION OF RELIGION

...

Paradoxically, his views have had an unanticipated influence on religious conservatives as well, who maintain that secular humanism is a religion and who quote John Dewey to make their case. They do so in part in order to exclude things they don't like from public schools—labeling them "secular humanist." For if humanism, even naturalistic and secular humanism, is a religion, then we would be faced with a violation of the First Amendment to the United States Constitution, which states that "Congress shall make no law respecting the establishment of religion or the free exercise thereof." This effort at redefining religion in such a way that not only religious humanism but also secular humanism become religious turns language upside down; like Lewis Carroll's Alice-in-Wonderland, conservatives seek by arbitrary fiat to make words mean whatever they want. Following this definition, atheism, as well as theism, is religious; but then virtually anything and everything may function religiously, and all distinctions collapse. In my judgement Dewey's use of religious language leads to unnecessary obfuscation.

...

80

HUMANISM IN THE FUTURE

...

Meaning of Life. Eupraxophy Centers will need to focus on eupraxia, good practice. They should deal with questions concerning the meaning of life, presupposing that the examined life *is* worth living. Once a person is liberated from the theistic world view and once he can use objective methods of inquiry, his next task is to find creative sources for meaningful expression. This task may very well become a central starting point for the Center. Many people are at sea, lost in a maze of misinformation, unable to make sense out of their personal lives, mired in confusion and despair. Not able to find themselves or to decide what they wish to get our of life, they flounder unmotivated and uncertain about which occupation or career they wish to enter or what they should do with their lives.

The humanist eupraxopher has adopted a life stance. He has clarified his first principle of ethics. He is aware of what he cherishes most in life. Thus, central to the educational mission of the Center can be the theory and practice of ethics, with special focus on practice. The Center can provide an environment in which moral dilemmas can be discussed openly and honestly—euthanasia, abortion, divorce, sexual morality, war and peace, the ethics of nuclear power, male and female roles, and so on. These questions can be debated without dogma or indoctrination, using the best critical

148

> "For if humanism, even naturalistic and secular humanism, is a religion, then we would be faced with a violation of the First Amendment to the United States Constitution, which states that "Congress shall make no law respecting the establishment of religion or the free exercise thereof.""

Exhibit 41

1990

STUDENT
HANDBOOK
1990-1991

THE UNIVERSITY OF
ARIZONA
TUCSON ARIZONA

**" Religious
Services
. . .
Humanists "**

{ RELIGIOUS
SERVICES

Religious services are offered by the various religious denominations located around the campus. Below is a list of these organizations, most of which are within walking distance of campus.

For a complete list of religious services, consult the Yellow Pages of the telephone directory under "Churches."

Ambassadors for Christ
2848 North Mountain Avenue
555-6053

American Baptist Campus Ministry
Campus Christian Center
715 North Park Avenue
555-7575

Baha'i Community of Tucson
Geology Building 105C
555-6044

Baptist Student Union
901 North Tyndall
555-4236

Beal Center
1030 North Mountain Avenue
555-9277

Campus Crusade for Christ
3524 N Charter Oak Way
555-0581

Chi Alpha
SUPO Box 20808
555-5259

Christian Science Organization
3915 N Campbell Avenue #96
555-3154

The Church of Jesus Christ of
Latter-Day Saints
1333 East Second Street
555-4204

Episcopal Campus Ministry
715 North Park Avenue
555-7575

Hillel Foundation
1245 East Second Street
555-6561

Humanists
PAS 342
555-6795
}

International Student Fellowship
2011 E 2nd Street
555-0332

Intervarsity Christian Fellowship
2651 N Santa Rita Avenue
555-2767

Islamic Center at Tucson
Gould-Simpson 123
555-6001

Little Chapel of All Nations
1052 North Highland
555-1692

Lutheran Campus Ministry
715 North Park Avenue
555-7575

The Navigators
915 N Tyndall Avenue

40

41

Only one of the religious groups listed in this directory can legally teach its doctrines in America's public schools: the Secular Humanists.

Exhibit 42

1991

The Origins of Modern Humanism

Edwin H. Wilson

The Humanist
January/February 1991
Pp. 9-11, 28.

. . .

If *secular* is defined as "not under God," the signers of the manifesto—who washed their hands of the supernatural, saying, "The time has passed for theism"—were all secularists. However, secular versus religious humanism is a false issue. By doing some homework—specifically, by reading Julian Huxley's *Religion without Revelation* or John Dewey's *A Common Faith*—we could do much to dissolve this divisive issue among humanists. . . .

28   The Humanist

Because the present interpretation of the First Amendment seeks removal of all religions from the public square, a few modern Humanists would like to abandon the use of the word "religious" to describe their worldview. Edwin H. Wilson takes these Humanists to task, however, by reminding them that Humanist leaders throughout history have understood their worldview to be religious.

Exhibit 43

1991

Commentary

VOLUME 92   NUMBER TWO   *AUGUST 1991*

The Future of American Jewry

———

Irving Kristol

[Pp. 21-26]

. . .

When we look at secularization without an ideological *parti pris*, we can fairly—and more accurately, I would suggest—describe it as the victory of a new, emergent religious impulse over the traditional biblical religions that formed the framework of Western civilization. Nor is there any mystery as to the identity of this new religious impulse. It is named, fairly and accurately, secular humanism. Merely because it incorporates the word "secular" in its self-identification does not mean that it cannot be seriously viewed as a competitive religion—though its adherents resent and resist any such ascription. Such resentment and resistance are, of course, a natural consequence of seeing the human world through "secularist" spectacles. Because secular humanism has, from the very beginning, incorporated the modern scientific view of the universe, it has always felt itself—and today still feels itself—"liberated" from any kind of religious perspective. But secular humanism is more than science, because it proceeds to make all kinds of inferences about the human condition and human possibilities that are not, in any authentic sense, scientific. Those inferences are metaphysical, and in the end theological.

There really is such a thing as secular humanism. The fact that many fundamentalist Protestants attack it in a mindless way, making it a kind of shibboleth, does not mean that it is, as some have been blandly saying, a straw man. It is not a straw man. . . .

It is secular humanism that is the orthodox metaphysical-theological basis of the two modern political philosophies, socialism and liberalism. The two are continuous across the secular-humanist spectrum, with socialism being an atheistic, messianic extreme while liberalism is an agnostic, melioristic version. (This continuity explains why modern liberalism cannot help viewing its disagreement with socialism—with the "Left"—as a kind of family quarrel.) Nor is it only modern politics that has been so shaped. Christianity and Judaism have been infiltrated and profoundly influenced by the spirit of secular humanism. . . .

[Pp. 22-23]

Irving Kristol's essay makes it clear that the religion of Secular Humanism is a serious threat to both the Jewish and Christian communities.

“It is secular humanism that is the orthodox metaphysical-theological basis of the two modern political philosophies, socialism and liberalism.”

— from page 23

Exhibit 44

1991

The international secular humanist magazine

Free Inquiry

Fall 1991   Vol. 11, No. 4 $5.00

Medicine:

**The Goodness of Planned Death
An Interview with
Dr. Jack Kevorkian**

. . .

Many right-wing fundamentalists insist that humanism is a religion, and that, therefore, the teaching of secularism or humanism in the public schools violates the First Amendment of the Constitution, and that secular humanism has to be extirpated. We in CODESH deny that secular humanism is a religion, and we think that the teaching of science, evolution, and humanistic values has an appropriate place in the public schools and in public life. . . .

50   FREE INQUIRY

. . .

In 1941 the American Humanist Association (AHA) was founded by Edwin Wilson, a Unitarian minister. Editor of the *Humanist* magazine, he attempted to defend nontheistic "religious humanism." There have been continuing battles in the AHA between those who wish a thoroughly naturalistic and secularized view of humanism (especially Sidney Hook and Corliss Lamont, who differed with Dewey's distinction between "religious" and "religion") and those who wish to emphasize the religious character of humanism. The AHA has never had more than three to five thousand members at its peak, and, like the AEU, has in recent years stagnated in membership. AHA still retains its religious exemption, despite an erroneous 1990 announcement that its tax status had changed; in any event AHA continues to emphasize that its Counsellor program is religious and performs "pastoral" and "ministerial" duties.

. . .

50   FREE INQUIRY

Paul Kurtz, author of *Humanist Manifesto II*, also authored the above article, "The Two Humanisms in Conflict: Religion vs. Secular." While Kurtz attempts to distance Secular Humanism from religion in this article, he makes three specific points: 1) The American Humanist Association is a 501(c)3 religious tax-exempt organization; 2) Humanistic ethics "has an appropriate place in the public schools"; 3) Kurtz used to teach that Secular Humanism "could become the religion of the future." The possibility that Humanist dogma may be banned from the public schools has since caused Kurtz to change his mind, and to deny the religious nature of his worldview.

. . .

For a long time I followed a path similar to Radest's. I held that humanism could become the religion of the future, and that, as such, it could inspire a "religious commitment." I was profoundly mistaken in that view. I think that it is time that humanism strike out anew and resist obfuscation with religious language. This is the task of CODESH and FREE INQUIRY.

. . . Humanism is more than social protest, more than an intellectual, political, or ethical agenda. It must speak to the private soliloquies of each and every person—and we need biographies of what it has meant in the lives of individual humanists.

Radest's final plea in his book I find both eloquent and meaningful:

> It is the radical claim of humanism that we can live rich and full lives while denying eternity. It is the even more radical claim that such lives are more satisfying precisely because they come closer to truthfulness and do not rely on illusions.(p. 159)

To which, I say, "Amen."

Exhibit 45

1993

HARVARD UNIVERSITY

Gazette

July 9, 1993   Vol. LXXXVIII   No. 42

INSIDE

■ Books: The Harvard University Press brings out a fall list that spans disciplines **Page 3**

■ Q&A: Office for Information Technology Director Stephen Hall on the future of computing **Page 5**

■ Exhibition: The Fogg Museum highlights great achievements of American modern art **Page 13**

Humanist Chaplain Serves Ethical 'Nonbelievers'

By Debra Bradley Ruder
Gazette Staff

As the Humanist chaplain at Harvard, Thomas Ferrick has a huge following: the entire University. Unfortunately, many people don't even know he exists.

"In a way, I have the largest constituency of any chaplain here," said Ferrick. "Harvard is a great secular university dedicated to truth and learning, and a majority of students, faculty, and staff lead decent, balanced, tolerant lives based on rational decisions. But few people are aware that humanism has summed up the wisdom of that life in its principles."

Ferrick, a former Catholic Priest, has held the Humanist chaplaincy since the position was established in 1975. Today, he is one of 34 full- and part-time chaplains that make up the United Ministry at Harvard and Radcliffe, and he also serves as executive director of the Humanist Association of Massachusetts' local chapter.

Yet his chaplaincy stands apart from the others, as it serves "nonbelievers with ethical principles and formed consciences."

Humanism is an approach to life—some call it a philosophy or religion—that values human experience, reason, logic, and scientific inquiry, according to Ferrick. It emphasizes the well-being of humans as a whole and as

(Continued on page 10)

> Thomas Ferrick, Humanist chaplain at Harvard. "Harvard is a great secular university dedicated to truth and learning, and a majority of students, faculty, and staff lead decent, balanced, tolerant lives based on rational decisions. But few people are aware that humanism has summed up the wisdom of that life in its principles."

Just as Christian or Muslim students need a chaplain to minister to them, so do students who adhere to the Humanist worldview. Such religious services are provided for Humanist students at Auburn University, the University of Arizona, and Harvard University. Chaplain Thomas Ferrick, who was supported by both the American Humanist Association and Corliss Lamont, admits that Secular Humanist teaching permeates the classroom at Harvard.

> **❝[T]hese students . . . are being constantly reinforced in their humanist beliefs in the classroom.❞**

Humanist Chaplain: Compassionate Counsel, 'Resident Skeptic'

(Continued from page 1)

individuals, and it recognizes that humans are flawed but open to improvement.

"Humanism is secularism at its very best," Ferrick explained in a recent interview. "It begins in the real world and tends to stress tolerance, patience, and respect for other human beings and for nature." Truth, to humanists "comes from the nitty-gritty of ordinary life—not from above—and from learning the consequences of our actions. In the last analysis, human beings are responsible for all their choices."

Although humanist organizations such as his are small, humanist principles are paramount in our nation's founding documents and in its courts, hospitals, laboratories, and universities, said Ferrick. The movement dates back to the ancient Greeks, flourished during the Enlightenment with such figures as Locke, Jefferson, Voltaire, and peaked in the 19th century with Darwin.

Over the years, Ferrick has collaborated with his colleagues in the United Ministry on many social-action issues. He also has worked to broaden the Ministry's membership to include more world religions such as Hinduism and Islam, and to revise its bylaws to reflect greater pluralism and equity.

Yet, the 64-year-old considers himself the "odd man out" because of his avowed atheism, independent ethics, and questioning.

"He's our resident skeptic," said Mary Karen Powers, a chaplain with the Catholic Student Center. "He never takes religious language or imagery at face value, and he pushes people to think about what they mean by the language they use. It's an important function for a chaplain to perform."

Although he speaks forcefully at times, "he's a very compassionate person who responds to people's physical, emotional, or spiritual pain in ways that are both kind and patient," Powers added. "He is concerned

about issues of justice. And he is very well-read and likes to talk about what he's read."

In fact, Ferrick's office in the basement of the Memorial Church doubles as a library containing 525 books—they're all cataloged—by well-known humanists such as Issac Asimov, Erich Fromm, and Linus Pauling. They bear titles such as *Losing Faith in Faith, God's Bullies,* and *What on Earth is an Atheist?*

A Personal Evolution

Ferrick's journey into and out of the priesthood is one of faith, disillusionment, and hope.

Orphaned at the age of 7, he grew up with a foster family in Massachusetts and attended the Jesuit-run Holy Cross College on a scholarship.

To no one's great surprise, Ferrick decided in 1951 to enter the seminary, studying at St. John's in Brighton.

That's where the trouble began.

"I was a bit of a nuisance in class, asking some difficult questions and not being satisfied with the answers," recalled Ferrick, still outspoken but very warm.

The young priest challenged the Church's treatment of women and homosexuals, its teachings about sexuality, and what he considered its undemocratic style. Later, he questioned the notions of original sin and redemption, preferring the scientific explanations about human evolution and behavior offered by Darwin.

During the 1960s, Ferrick served as Catholic chaplain at Dartmouth College, where he gave sermons against the Vietnam War and was active in the civil rights movement, and then at Boston State College.

The "worst blow of all" to his faith in the Church came in the late 1960s, when Pope Paul VI forbade the use of birth control, said Ferrick, a firm believer in a woman's reproductive rights and in population control.

"This was, I thought, a crime against humanity—and I still do," he said. "It was a clear sign to me of a fundamental imperfection of the Church. So, I resigned."

Meanwhile, a professor had introduced Ferrick to the Ethical Culture Society, a branch of humanism that emphasizes ethical behavior, human relationships, and deed over creed.

After serving as a leader-in-training in St. Louis for three years, Ferrick returned to the East Coast and became leader of the Boston Ethical Society.

When that position's funding dried up, he approached three national organizations—the American Humanist Association, the American Ethical Union, and the Fellowship of Religious Humanists—to see whether they would support a humanist chaplaincy at Harvard. They agreed, and Ferrick has held the job ever since.

He sought to establish the chaplaincy because "I thought that all college students could use the counsel, ethical teaching, and frame of reference that a humanist provides," Ferrick said. "I also believed that a University, as a community, needs that kind of ministry."

"I knew Harvard was forever fighting the temptations of power, greed, and selfishness," he remembered. "This is the other, darker side of success; the good life has to be balanced. Harvard has some moral dilemmas to confront."

Today, the full-time position is funded by generous gifts from Corliss Lamont '24 and the Humanist Association of Massachusetts, as well as smaller donations and fees from weddings and memorial services. Ferrick said he manages on a salary of less than $15,000 because he is single and maintains a modest lifestyle. To ensure the longevity of the chaplaincy, though, the board of directors—all Harvard alumni—recently created an endowment fund.

The Chaplain's Role

As chaplain, Ferrick—who has a master's degree in counseling—advises students and others about personal or family troubles, career choices, and questions of ethics and philosophy.

When first-year students voluntarily indi-

cate their religious affiliations during registration each year, fewer than 200 check off humanism, said Ferrick.

Moreover, only a fraction of those actually seek his guidance. That may be because "humanist students do not relate to their religious or ethical figures the way other students relate to theirs," he said. "As a nonauthority figure, I'm not as needed. Not only do these students require less guidance, but they are being constantly reinforced in their humanist beliefs in the classroom."

With growing frequency, Ferrick is called upon by the Memorial Church to perform weddings and memorial services for Harvard people who are not religious "but who see this edifice as a moral center within the University community," he explained.

The chaplain also produces a monthly newsletter, and the chapter offers a regular program of speakers on such morally vexing topics as doctor-assisted suicide, abortion, and energy consumption. They attract anywhere between 50 and several hundred people.

In addition, Ferrick has expanded the list of *holy days* issued by Harvard to include three *holidays* he considers worth celebrating by humanists: Free Thinkers Day (Oct. 12), International Human Rights Day (Dec. 25), and Earth Day (March 20).

"As an organization, we have wonderful ideals, but our achievements are relatively modest," he said. "We're bucking traditional ways and attitudes that take a long time to turn around.

"People, it seems to me, are much more humanistic in their thinking than in their behavior," Ferrick reflected. "For most, life is difficult and we don't measure up to our own ideals; otherwise, we wouldn't allow substandard living in our urban ghettos, or the proliferation of guns in our society. . . . We need more heroes like Andrei Sakharov, a remarkably honest man and one of this era's great humanists. We need to be more selfless, we need to overcome our individualism and think more about community and our common destiny."

page 10

Exhibit 46
1994

Religious Life at Harvard 1994 - 95

United Ministry at Harvard & Radcliffe
Memorial Church, Harvard Yard
Cambridge, MA 02138
(617) 495-5529

HILLEL FOUNDATION (Jewish)

Harvard/Radcliffe Hillel serves as the center for Jewish student life on campus. An active Student Board and fourteen different Student Committees plan and implement social and cultural activities, lectures, programs, social service projects, and leadership training. Hillel is host to five worship communities, the Institute of Jewish Studies and the Kosher Food Program for the University. A strong sense of friendship is the hallmark of this student-run community. Address: The Riesman Center, 52 Mt. Auburn St., Cambridge, MA 02138

- Rabbi Sally Finestone 495-4696
- Rabbi Ben-Zion Gold 495-4696
- Rabbi Harry Sinoff 495-4696
- Dr. Benard Steinberg 495-4696

HUMANIST CHAPLAINCY

This ministry celebrates humanity in its earthly and evolutionary context. Its appeal is to the skeptical inquirer, the idealistic student of an agnostic or atheistic inclination. It's for those who prize the scientific, aesthetic, and democratic achievements of human beings, past and present. A Humanist values knowledge over faith, and deed before creed, rejoices in differences and variety, and is comfortable with ambiguity. Lectures and seminars are held regularly; easy conversation anytime. A library of books and journals is available to all inquirers, along with coffee and a warm welcome. Recently some Humanist students have formed an organization: The Free Thought Society of Harvard University. The Chaplaincy's Board of Directors is drawn from the Harvard Alumni. Mailing address: United Ministry, Memorial Church, Harvard Yard.

- Thomas M. Ferrick 495-5529 (o), 547-1497 (h)

INTERVARSITY CHRISTIAN FELLOWSHIP

InterVarsity Christian Fellowship is an interdenominational evangelical Christian ministry for undergraduate and graduate students. We work with the *Harvard Radcliffe Christian Fellowship* (HRCF) and with the *Graduate School Christian Fellowship* (GSCF), which includes groups at each of the graduate and professional schools. Weekly meetings are held for worship, prayer and Bible study. We sponsor retreats, participate in community service projects, and offer short term mission experiences. Study discussions are available for those interested in exploring the

[n.p.]

The booklet, published by Harvard University's United Ministry, entitled, "Religion at Harvard 1995-96," places "Humanist Chaplaincy" between a Jewish group (Hillel Foundation) and a Christian Group (InterVarsity Christian Fellowship). Humanism is rightly recognized as religious in character and function.

Exhibit 47

1995

STUDENT ORGANIZATIONS

Office of Student Activities

. . .

Office of Student Activities
Minneapolis Campus   St. Paul Campus
256 Coffman Union   190 Coffey Hall
Minneapolis, MN 55455   St. Paul, MN 55108
(612) 624-5101   (612) 625-9225

Office of the Vice President for Student Affairs
UNIVERSITY OF MINNESOTA

11/09/95 12:54 PM

. . .

Religious

African Christian Union of MN Victor Weir 1017 Raymond Ave #11 St. Paul, MN 55108 645-6937.
B'Nai Brith Hillel Foundation Dana Zickerman 1521 University Ave SE Minneapolis, MN 55414 379-4026.
Bahi Association Mahtab Rezai 21905 Minnetonka Blvd Excelsior, MN 55331 474-0483.
Buddhist Assocation Vincent Kuo PO Box 14337 Minneapolis, MN 55414 378-3957.
Baptist Student Union Yis Vang 1127 Edmund Ave St. Paul, MN 55104 644-5883.
Campus Advance Todd Viegut 810 Thornton St SE #1105 Minneapolis, MN 55414 341-0992.
Campus Ambassadors Dave Scully 874 22nd Ave Minneapolis, MN 55414 379-9167.
Campus Crusade for Christ Steve Peterson 1120`-5th St SE Minneapolis, MN 55414 379-7151.
Cantonese Christian Fellowship Esther Yam 621 5th Ave #20 Minneapolis, MN 55414.
CARP Eric Richardson 1000 5th St SE Minneapolis, MN 55414 378-1416.
Catholic Student Assoc Kristofer Spong 1701 University Ave SE Minneapolis, MN 55414 331-3437.
Chinese Christian Campus Flwshp Chi Sing Lee PO Box 14967 Minneapolis, MN 55414 379-4483.
Christian Legal Society/U of M Law School Brenda VanRaalte 285 Law Center Minneapolis, MN 55455 788-3893.
Christian Medical/Dental Society Jason Dahuburg 3508 Glen Arden St Paul, MN 55112 633-1961.
Christian Science Organization Jill Jackson 803 S.E. Huron St. Minneapolis, MN 55414 338-0472.
Christian Student Fellowship Christopher Minor 1515 Brook Ave SE Minneapolis, MN 55414 378-2657.
Christians in Action Michael laczek 310 18th Ave SE Minneapolis, MN 55414 379-3021.
Eckankar on Campus Rick Duffy 2432 Humboldt Ave S Minneapolis, MN 55405 377-9238.
Episcopal Student Association Mark Ott 317 17th Ave SE Minneapolis, MN 55414 331-3552.
Good News for Israel Valerie Voelker P.O. Box 23018 Richfield, MN 55423 378-3862.
Graduate Christian Fellowship Stacey Hecht 10551 Greenbrier Rd #371 Minnetonka, MN 55305 525-1724.
Haiyay Shalom Bible Fellowship Valerie Voelker 4728 Vincent Ave So Menneapolis, MN 55410 831-0284.
Indonesian Christian Fellowship Suwipin Martono 1901 Minnehaha Ave #418 Minneapolis, MN 55404 673-0934.
Intervarsity Christian Fellowship Marci Peterson 501 Oak St SE Minneapolis, MN 55414 331-3552.
International Student Friendship Ministries Robert Chambers 310 18th Ave SE Minneapolis, MN 55414 379-3021.
Latter-Day Saints Students Assoc Amy Bryans 1205 University Ave SE Minneapolis, MN 55414 331-1154.
Lighthouse Patrick Conley 501 Oak St SE Minneapolis, MN 55414 31-1632.
Lutheran Campus Ministry Jonahan Yang 317 17th Ave SE Minneapolis, MN 55414 331-3552.
Lutheran Student Fellowship Derek Roberts 1101 University Ave SE Minneapolis, MN 55414 331-2747.
Lutheran Student Movement Tracie Wahlberg 317 17th Ave SE Minneapolis, MN 55414 378-2299.
Meditations Club Hong Zeng 1211 Fifield Ave St. Paul, MN 55108 645-0037.
Maranatha Christian Fellowship Paul Appelget 315 10th Ave SE Minneapolis, MN 55414 378-2299.
Muslim Student Association Ahmad Azizi 235 Coffman Minneapolis Campus 624-5656.
New Life Erica Wnukowski 2333 Priscilla St #8 St. Paul, MN 551-8 603-0313.
Nurses Christian Fellowship Jennifer Pieper 6-101 HSUF Minneapolis Campus, MN 55414 624-5656
Orthodox Christian Fellowship Tim Richardson 1037 29th Ave SE #E Minneapolis, MN 55414 378-4884.
St. Paul Campus Bible Study Fellowship Brian Bostrom 567 37th Ave. NE Columbia Heights 789-8986.
Toshavim Cecil Smith 720 13th Ave S Minneapolis, MN 55415 338-7653.
{   **U of M Atheists and Humanists** Catalina Chadbourn 235 Coffman Union Minneapolis Campus 379-4786.
University Unitarian Universalists Mike Burns 1511 Rollins Ave Minneapolis, MN 55455 623-7884.
Women of Virtue Renee Meyer 315 10th Ave SE Minneapolis, MN 55414 378-3862.

. . .

"Religious . . . U of M Atheists and Humanists "

The University of Minnesota's "Student Organizations" listing, provided by the Office of the Vice President, naturally placed the "U of M Atheists and Humanists" under the "Religious" organizations. As of July 13, 1999, they have been assigned under the "Political and Social Action" section. This was truly a political action, possibly due to its being used as evidence in the article noted in Exhibit 49.

Peninsula

May 1996   Volume 7, Number 3

Religion At Harvard

Exhibit 48

1996

❝Understanding the faith behind this chaplaincy . . . will bring you very close to understanding the religion of Harvard University.**❞**

❝ Mr. Ferrick, however, is comfortable in defining humanism as a "faith in the natural" — in particular, in the natural goodness of humanity. He admits that this faith cannot be proved rationally, particularly in the light of consistent crimes of human beings, but maintains that a humanist will nevertheless cling to a belief — or rather, a faith — in human intelligence and compassion.**❞**

Divine Aspirations
Humanism and Harvard

The United Ministry conducts its business at Harvard largely unnoticed in the lives of secular students—which is not surprising. It is somewhat more surprising that even students who take religious faith seriously have little contact with the United Ministry as such. They may meet a United Ministry chaplain, but probably it will happen because that particular chaplain also serves one of the Harvard Square churches. Students may never realize that the advisors to Christian Impact and Christian Fellowship, or the chaplains at the Catholic Students Association, as well as the rabbis at Hillel, are all members of the United Ministry.

The membership of the United Ministry, which is defined in its bylaws as a "voluntary organization of professional ministers of established faith communities which have constituencies among students, faculty, administration and staff at Harvard-Radcliffe", includes representatives of 24 different religious faiths. This is no more than appropriate, because Harvard students hold a wide variety of religious beliefs. Still, a large number of students at Harvard do not profess a religious faith—and even for these students, there is representation in the United Ministry. Since 1975, Thomas Ferrick has held the position of "Humanist Chaplain" on the United Ministry. Understanding the faith behind this chaplaincy, and the form that that faith takes, will bring you very close to understanding the religion of Harvard University. Indeed, the humanist chaplaincy might well be referred to as the heart of Harvard.

To a student running an eye down the list of United Ministry chaplains, it seems peculiar to see "Humanism" listed among the names of religious groups. Ferrick's claim that humanism at Harvard should be defined as a "faith community" is unusual. Not all humanists, who as a group like to emphasize rational investigation and scientific knowledge, would agree that their system of thought has a strong component of faith. Mr. Ferrick, however, is comfortable in defining humanism as a "faith in the natural"—in particular, in the natural goodness of humanity. He admits that this faith cannot be proved rationally, particularly in the light of consistent crimes of human beings, but maintains that a humanist will nevertheless cling to a belief—or rather, a faith—in human intelligence and compassion.

Students at Harvard obviously share this extremely optimistic view of human nature. Nor is this unusual for Americans in the modern world. During the nineteenth century, most Protestant denominations in the United States fought internal battles over the issue of original sin, in what some historians call the "decline of American Calvinism." Many of the great revivalists of the Second Great Awakening rejected predestination, origi-

nal sin, and infant damnation. This legacy remains with American churches in the 1990s, a time when churches almost never discuss that old-fashioned concept of "sin." And secular Americans are even more fervent believers in the ability of humanity to achieve peace and world harmony through the exertion of previously unrecognized depths of compassion and love. Thomas Ferrick sees this quality in most Harvard students: "Take a student," he says, "With a basically secular outlook, and add a sense of ethics and a caring about human beings—and that's a humanist."

The implication that religious students do not really have a sense of ethics, or do not really care about other human beings, seems accidental.

Because of its emphasis on creating a better world through human goodness, humanism at Harvard focuses a great deal on the ethical questions of modern life. These frequently take the form of ethical political questions. Thus, we come inevitably to the strong ties of the Humanist Chaplaincy to liberal politics.

The chaplaincy does not always sponsor speakers whose subjects are political. Within the past year, for example, one meeting was taken up with discussion of whether humanists are too likely to submerge emotion in the exercise of reason. However, many of the speakers sponsored by the chaplaincy are invited to discuss what Mr. Ferrick calls "ethical political questions."

A recent speaker sponsored by the humanist chaplaincy was Chip Berlet, speaking on "Right-Wing Populism: Scapegoating,

---

Thus we come inevitably to the strong ties of the Humanist Chaplaincy to liberal politics.

Militias, and the Buchanan Phenomonon." Berlet is one of the leaders of the Political Research Associates, a Central Square research group that tracks right-wing propaganda. Due to his detailed knowledge of militia movements, Mr. Berlet's presentation had a depth to it that is unusual in Harvard speakers dealing with subjects outside of the left wing. Unfortunately, some of the usual suspects sneaked into the speech anyway. The "conspiracy" by Christians to take over school boards was avowed, Pat Buchanan was termed irresponsible for his use of "code language." The "soft right," (meaning your ordinary everyday conservatives, as opposed to your militia types,) were

continued on p. 14

Harvard's student publication, *Peninsula* (May 1996), carried an article by P. Brown entitled "Humanism and Harvard." P. Brown observes that humanism at Harvard is treated as a religion. The Humanist Chaplain admits his worldview is a "faith."

127

> **"** . . . the pamphlet goes on to say, through its Legal Action Committee the AHA is fighting the religious right on all fronts—particularly in attempting to force the Boy Scouts to condone homosexuality by allowing homosexuals to serve as Scout Leaders, and discouraging even further any sensitivity toward religion that remains in public schools. **"**

Humanism, continued from p. 11

labelled the "theocratic" right, because "they want to impose their beliefs on everyone."

Nor is an event so focused on left-wing politics unusual for the Humanist chaplaincy. During the past year they have also had Representative Doug Peterson (Marblehead, MA) present a case for his proposed legislation in favor of assisted suicide. The speech was titled: "Assisted Suicide: Lessons Learnt from the Kevorkian Affair." Indeed, Mr. Ferrick notes that speeches regarding current events are more effective in drawing a crowd—but that they are always tailored to focus upon "ethical issues" within the political scene.

The implication that a speaker who argued that euthanasia was wrong would be taking an unethical position does not seem accidental at all. The view from the humanist left does not recognize the ethical dimensions of arguments from the religious right.

The speakers invited, logically, reflect the opinions of the humanist audience. This is fair enough—a Roman Catholic cleric would not be expected to invite speakers to address his flock that would contradict the teachings of the Roman Catholic Church. It is both obvious and to be expected that Harvard's humanist ministry partakes of the "progressive" biases and errors that characterize the American Humanist Association, by whom Mr. Ferrick is certified as a Humanist Counsellor. In a brochure titled "Impacting Society", distributed by the chaplaincy at the Berlet speech, the AHA outlines its "accomplishments" throughout the past thirty years. The list is truly a walk of shame:

> "During the 1960s, the American Humanist Association was the first national membership organization to endorse elective abortion...In 1974, long before the activism of Dr. Jack Kevorkian and the Hemlock Society, the National Commission for Beneficent Euthanasia was established as an AHA program..."

Currently, the pamphlet goes on to say, through its Legal Action Committee the AHA is fighting the religious right on all fronts—particularly in attempting to force the Boy Scouts to condone homosexuality by allowing homosexuals to serve as Scout Leaders, and discouraging even further any sensitivity toward religion that remains in public schools. In the same pamphlet, the AHA even claims Margaret Sanger (the founder of Planned Parenthood, who believed that birth control was necessary to stop blacks from taking over the cities) as one of its most distinguished forerunners. Moreover, the Humanist Manifesto II, a "consensus statement on social policy" for humanists, supports all of these positions, as well as "the development of a system of world law and a world order based on transnational federal government."

It is to be expected that a faith community, in this case a community with faith in humanity as a whole, would formulate for itself political beliefs. Religious conservatives will hardly dispute the rights of humanists to bring their religious beliefs into the political sphere. The right won't be snivelling about the separation of faith from politics when the American Humanist Association begins to push its agenda.

But in this case, it is difficult to see how humanism as a community unto itself exists outside its ties to a clearly defined political agenda.

It is this absence of meaning apart from liberal politics that makes a Humanist ministry so truly appropriate for Harvard. Humanism, with its faith in human goodness and centralized government, has indeed summarized the principles of many people in the Harvard community. And, as Mr. Ferrick said to the Harvard Gazette in an article of July 9, 1993, "[students] are being constantly reinforced in their humanist beliefs in the classroom." Students who still cling to a belief in a Deity, or even a Trinity, have only to look to Thomas Ferrick to find the religion of Harvard University.

-P. Brown

> **"** Students who still cling to a belief in a Deity, or even a Trinity, have only to look to Thomas Ferrick to find the religion of Harvard University. **"**

THE INTERNATIONAL SECULAR HUMANIST MAGAZINE

Free Inquiry

Fall 1996   Vol. 16, No. 4

Exhibit 49

Defining
HUMANISM
The Battle Continues...

The Religion of Secular Humanism

David A. Noebel

Religion: (1.) A worldview i.e., any set of beliefs or system of thought that contains a theology, philosophy, ethics, biology, psychology, sociology, economics, politics, law and history.—Noebel *(2.) "Among religions in this country which do not teach what would generally be considered a belief in the existence of God are Buddhism, Taoism, Ethical Culture, Secular Humanism and others."*—U.S. Supreme Court (1961) *(3.) "Any system of beliefs, practices, ethical values . . . [e.g.], humanism as a religion."*—Webster's New World Dictionary *(4.) "A system of thought shared by a group that gives members an object of devotion [God, the state, man, nature], a code of ethics and a frame of reference relating individuals to their group and the universe."*—Columbia Encyclopedia *(5.) "Secularism . . . is the name for an ideology, a new closed worldview which functions very much like a new religion."*—Harvey Cox *(6.) "Over the years, men and women who embrace the philosophy or faith known as Humanism have contributed significantly toward improving the condition of life for all."*—American Humanist Association *(7.) "Pure religion . . . is this, to visit the fatherless and widows in their affliction, and to keep oneself unspotted from the world."*—James (1:27)

Secular Humanism is a religion. It is a religion because it contains, as all

David A. Noebel, President of Summit Ministries, is the author of Clergy in the Classroom: The Religion of Secular Humanism *and* Understanding the Times: The Religious Worldviews of Our Day and the Search for Truth. *Summit Ministries supplements the education of Christian students attending non-Christian high schools, colleges, and universities.*

> "Secular Humanism is a religion. It is a religion because it contains, as all worldviews contain, a theology."

worldviews contain, a theology. When Paul Kurtz says in the 1973 *Humanist Manifesto* that "no deity will save us, we must save ourselves" he speaks the language of religion. Salvation is a religions experience and concept. While the Christian worldview insists that God (or Jesus Christ) alone can save our souls (regeneration) and bodies (resurrection), the secular humanist worldview insists that reason and science can save humanity through progressive governmental and liberal educational programs.

It is a religion because it possesses and promotes a religious symbol–a fish with feet and the name Darwin enscribed. The religious symbol of the Christian worldview is either the cross or the fish with the name Jesus enscribed.

But even more specific is Kurtz's own declaration in his preface to the Humanist *Manifestos I and II* that, "Humanism is a philosophical, religious and moral point of view." FREE INQUIRY Senior Editor Gerald A. Larue says that humanism is, "a religion to meet the psychological

needs of our time," and Edwin H. Wilson, the 1979 Humanist of the Year and former editor of *The Humanist*, says that, "Humanism in a naturalistic frame is validly a religion."

While I argue in *Understanding The Times: The Religious Worldviews of Our Day and the Search for Truth* that secular humanism is a comprehensive worldview that consists of a theology (atheism), philosophy (metaphysical naturalism), ethics (moral relativism), biology (spontaneous generation/evolution), psychology (self-actualization), sociology (feminism/homosexualism), law (positivism), politics (globalism), economics (socialism), and history (French Enlightenment II), Kurtz acknowledges the three main pillars of any worldview viz., theology, philosophy, and ethics.

One of the early voices of Secular Humanism was Charles Francis Potter. Potter signed the *Humanist Manifesto* (1933) along with John Dewey and Roy Wood Sellars. Potter was a Baptist minister for eleven years and a Unitarian minister for eleven more years before founding the first Humanist church in New York City in 1929. In Potter's 1930 book *Humanism: A New Religion* he states, "Humanism is not simply another denomination of Protestant Christianity; it is not a creed; nor is it a cult. It is a new type of religion altogether."

It is, as Roy Wood Sellars, author of the 1933 *Humanist Manifesto*, says, "A religion founded on realities in a religion coming of age." Sellars said this in his ground-breaking work *Religion Coming of Age* (1928).

Indeed, nearly all the early secular humanists admitted that secular humanism was a religion. John Dewey, for example, in his *A Common Faith* concluded his book by stating, "Here are all the elements for a religious faith that shall not be confined to sect, class, or race. Such a faith has always been implicitly the common faith of mankind. It remains to make it explicit and militant."

While the Humanist movement has made the faith explicit, the American educational establishment has made it militant. The religion of Secular Humanism is the only worldview allowed in the public schools. All other competing worldviews

In this article David A. Noebel summarizes the case that Secular Humanism is a religion. While other authors disagreed, sometimes quite forcefully, we believe the argument made in both this article and this book have not been successfully answered.

have been declared illegal by the U.S. Supreme Court and effectively eliminated bit by bit–1962 (prayer), 1963 (the Bible), 1980 (Ten Commandments), and 1987 (God).

Curtis W. Reese edited numerous volumes entitled *Humanist Sermons* and in 1931 wrote a work for the MacMillan publishing company entitled *Humanist Religion*. Reese had no problem with the notion that Secular Humanism was a religion. That problem came later when the Paul Kurtzes of the world began to realize that secular humanism was in danger of having to withdraw from the public education square under the same interpretation of the separation doctrine that Humanists cleverly used to eradicate Christianity from the public schools.

But that was yesterday. What about now? Basically nothing has changed. In fact, the evidence is stronger today that Secular Humanism is a religion than seventy-five years ago.

The 1994 Humanists of the Year, Lloyd and Mary Morain, co-authored a work in 1954 titled *Humanism as the Next Step: An Introduction for Liberal Protestants, Catholics, and Jews.* Chapter One was "The Fourth Faith." The Morains sincerely believe, as did Sellars, that secular humanism is the historically logical and rationally based religion to follow in the wake of the other three religions. Indeed, there are few differences between liberal or liberated Protestantism, Catholicism, Judaism, and Humanism! All speak and understand the language of theological creativity, ethical situationism, biological evolution, political correctness, sexual experimentation, and the "gospel" of tolerance and broadmindedness (except for Eastern Orthodox and Evangelicals).

The U.S. Supreme Court noted in *Torcasco v. Watkins* (1961) that secular humanism was indeed a religion in the same vein as other world religions like Buddhism and Taoism. When the U.S. Supreme Court identified secular humanism as a religion it did so, according to James Davison Hunter, by expanding the meaning of religion. At one time the Court used the term *religion* in its substantive form, e.g., *Davis v. Bacon* (1890) and (1892), but beginning in 1943 (*United States v. Kauten)* the Court began using a

functional definition of religion in order to include non-Christian and non-theistic religions. Secular humanism, for better or worse, falls under this nontheistic functional definition of religion. It is, in reality, a nontheistic, natural religion, with a naturalistic deity *viz.*, natural selection.

Secular humanist lawyer Leo Pfeffer wrote in a 1977 issue of the *Journal of Church & State* that secular humanism would triumph over three religions–Protestantism, Catholicism, and Judaism. His article "The Triumph of Secular Humanism" makes it clear that Humanism is not merely a philosophical or political movement. Only religions triumph over other religions. Only faiths triumph over other faiths.

Paul Kurtz, writing in the Winter 1986/ 87 issue of FREE INQUIRY, admits that the organized humanist movement is put in a quandry over the question of religion. Why? Because the Fellowship of Religious Humanists, the American Ethical Union, the Society for Humanistic Judaism, and the American Humanist Association "all consider themselves to be religious." Indeed, Kurtz laments the fact that the American Humanist Association has "a religious tax exemption" (p. 5). [This has since changed.–EDS.]

In a follow-up article on the same subject (FREE INQUIRY, Fall 1991) Kurtz states that the American Humanist Association "still retains its religious exemption . . . [and] continues to emphasize that is Counselor program is religious and performs 'pastoral' and 'ministerial' duties" (p. 5).

Secular humanist groups on our nation's campuses are routinely placed in the religious sections of student directories. For example, in the Auburn University student and faculty directory for 1985/86 under "Auburn Pastors and Campus Ministries" one finds the Humanists listed with Dr. Delos McKown as "Humanist Counselor." McKown, a contributing editor for FREE INQUIRY magazine, wears two hats at Auburn–philosophy professor and humanist priest.

In the University of Arizona student handbook for 1990/91, the "Humanists" are listed alongside of Ambassadors for Christ, American Baptist Campus Ministry, Baptist Student Union, Campus Crusade for Christ, etc. At the University

of Minnesota the "U of M Atheists and Humanists" are identified under "Student Organizations–Religious." Listed with "U of M Atheists and Humanists" are such groups as the Buddhist Association, Baptist Student Union, Campus Crusade for Christ, Catholic Student Association, Muslim Student Association, University Unitarian Universalists, and Women of Virtue.

Writing in the August 1991 issue of *Commentary* magazine, Irving Kristol identifies secular humanism as the "new religious impulse" that stands in contrast to "the traditional biblical religions that formed the framework of Western civilization." Kristol argues that this new religious impulse "is more than science" since it makes all kinds of inferences about the human condition and human possibilities. He insists that this religion of secular humanism is "the orthodox metaphysical-theological basis of the two modern political philosophies, socialism and liberalism."

But let me conclude with an example from Harvard. The *Harvard University Gazette* (July 9, 1993) contained a front-page article by Debra Bradley Ruder entitled, "Humanist Chaplain Serves Ethical 'Nonbelievers.'" The chaplain, Thomas Ferrick, is one of thirty-four full- and part-time chaplains at Harvard and Radcliffe, and serves as executive director of the Humanist Association of Massachusetts. Ferrick, a former Roman Catholic priest, left the priesthood over the issues of evolution and homosexuality, to take up the Humanist chaplaincy at Harvard.

Ferrick's support comes from the American Humanist Association, the American Ethical Union, the Fellowship of Religious Humanists, the Humanist Association of Massachusetts and Dr. Corliss Lamont. Lamont, who died last year, was the author of *The Philosophy of Humanism* and frequent writer for *The Humanist* magazine and even FREE INQUIRY. For Corliss Lamont, a long-time, hard-core, true Humanist believer, to financially support a Humanist chaplain at Harvard and help establish an endowment fund for such a chaplaincy speaks volumes about the true nature of Secular Humanism.

The *Gazette* article states that

8

Harvard's first-year students can voluntarily indicate their "religious affiliations during registration." Says Chaplain Ferrick, "fewer than 200 check off humanism."

But, as the article concludes, "Only a fraction of those students actually seek his guidance. That may be because 'humanist students to not elate to their religious or ethical figures the way other students

relate to theirs.' Not only do these students require less guidance, but they are being constantly reinforced in their humanist beliefs in the classroom."

I rest my case.

References

Dewey, John, *A Common Faith* (New Haven: Yale University Press, 1934), p. 87.

Kurtz, Paul, "Preface," *Humanist Manifestoes I and II* (Prometheus, 1973) p. 16.
Kurtz, Paul, "Preface," *Humanist Manifestoes I and II* (Prometheus, 1973) p. 3
Pfeffer, Leo, "The Triumph of Secular Humanism," *Journal of Church and State* 1977, p. 211.
Potter, Charles Francis, *Humanism:A New Religion* (New York: Simon & Schuster, 1930) p.3.
Sellars, Roy Wood, *Religion Coming of Age* (New York: Macmillan) 1928) p. vi.
Wilson, Edwin, "Humanism's Many Dimensions," in *The Humanist Alternative*, ed. Paul Kurtz, (Prometheus, 1973) p. 15.

9

130

Exhibit 50

1998

ACCESS TO ENERGY

A Pro-Science, Pro-Technology, Pro-Free Enterprise Monthly Newletter

DECEMBER 1998 (Vol. 26, no. 4)   Box1250, Cave Junction, Oregon 97523   Copyright © 1998 by *Access to Energy*

State Sponsored Religion

My daughter Arynne was very nearly thrown out of Southern Oregon University (SOU), a tax-financed school near here, midway through her first quarter as a college student this past month. After a serious argument with University officials, she is being permitted to complete the academic year – but has been told, in no uncertain terms, not to return as a student next year.

Arynne is a shy 18-year-old girl who enrolled in September and is taking calculus, physics, chemistry (all at the 200, sophomore level) and organ classes. She made the honor roll first quarter with grades of A in calculus, physics, and organ, and B in chemistry. It is true that Arynne lacks the drugs; alcohol; sexual promiscuity; nose, ear, and tongue rings; tatoos; arrogant lack of respect for older adults; dishonesty; and profanity of speech that are characteristic of many of her fellow students. Her demeanor is recognizably different as a result. Arynne's lack of these social graces is not, however, the reason that university officials first demanded that she leave after one quarter – and ultimately agreed to allow her to finish the year (she is taking three-quarter courses) before departing.

Arynne's sin is that she has refused to take the University's three-quarter, four-unit per quarter (out of 15 units in the usual course load) total-immersion indoctrination course in the Oregon State Religion.

This course is a mandatory requirement for any student to be on the campus and take courses–regardless of whether or not he seeks a degree. (It is, of course, required for graduation, too.) Arynne's brother Noah attends the same university, but he skipped the course with advanced placement. Arynne entered taking a full load of science and math. An apparent mistake by university officials allowed her to do so without taking the religious indoctrination course.

When a priestess in the "Student ACCESS Center" discovered this, she initiated an investigation. Arynne was told to drop one of her science of math courses and take the religion course – or else be expelled from the University after one term. Actually, the priestess wanted Arynne to drop calculus and enroll in the religion course in the middle of the first term – at the time Arynne's sin was discovered.

Arynne and Noah are attending this university for two reasons. It is close to home (one and one-half hour drive), and it has an excellent undergraduate science program. The science faculty is devoted to undergraduate education (they do not have a graduate school) and has developed a four-year program that provides first-class courses in all of the necessary subjects. SOU also has an excellent music program. As in most universities today, however, the humanities departments and administrators – not the scientists – control the campus.

Imagine the outcry if a tax-financed state university required every student to take, as a condition of being on the campus, a full-year course in Christianity and Biblical studies – that included giving speeches, writing essays, participating in discussion groups, and developing "critical thinking skills" (SOU's terminology) necessary to understand and appreciate the value of being a Christian.

To be sure, SOU bills this course as a speech, writing, and "critical thinking" course. SOU does not, however, allow any of its better (and far more value-neutral) courses involving speech and writing to be substituted for it.

The course text for "Colloquium," the mandatory course, is a collection of articles chosen by the SOU humanities faculty and printed specially for this course. It is devoted primarily to the teaching of the university's own brand of atheistic secular humanism – including radical feminism, non-absolute morals, situational ethics (if it feels good, do it), and atheistic existentialism.

Aha, you say, just a philosophy course – not a bad idea for students to be familiar with different philosophies. No, the text does not contain a single work by any significant historian, author, or educator. Several of the essays are about education, but the only immediately recognizable author among them is Malcolm X. Students are asked to write and speak about the educational philosophy of Malcolm X.

Malcolm X qualified for the text, no doubt, because he was a racist, advocate of violence, and felon. Booker T. Washington – a truly great black educator who overcame personal challenges of race that were orders of magnitude more severe than those encountered by Malcolm X – is not mentioned, but then Booker T. Washington was not a racist, did not advocate violence, and was not a felon.

Arynne's real sin, of course, is that she is a Christian. She is quite tolerant of people with all sorts of views, but she is not willing to take a total-immersion, one-year course in atheism and its currently popular, politically correct manifestations. This is not a survey course. In order to receive a passing grade, she would be required – for a full academic year – to read, write, give speeches, engage in indoctrination discussions, and answer "correctly" examination questions – primarily devoted to religious beliefs entirely opposite to her own.

Moreover, this brew of New-Age, New-Left, politically correct psychobabble is not conducive to her study of science. Speech and writing experience is helpful in many pursuits – but not when it is obtained at the expense of forced pseudo-rational indoctrination.

The Oregon State Religion being promulgated here is indeed different from other religions. A great religion emphasizes the higher human traits. The Oregon religion is based primarily upon the lowest aspects of human nature. (The course text opens with a 13-page article on rape, including detailed descriptions of actual rapes – which sets the stage for teaching feminism – and goes downhill from there.)

It is not unusual to have all sorts of courses on a college campus. Increasingly, some particularly objectionable ones are being required for graduation. (Zachary was forced to take, as a graduation requirement at Oregon State University, a "health" class that was so raw his 45-year-old-male chemistry advisor was too embarrassed to discuss its contents with him. Zachary and some of his fellow students simply walked out of some degraded presentations by the woman "professor" teaching this course.) It is new, however, to require indoctrination courses *as a condition of being physically on the campus at all as a student* regardless of the question of receiving a degree.

As a science, technology, freedom, and the mores of Western civilization are increasingly ripped apart in American society, it is evident that our tax-financed universities are doing their best to participate.

The editor of *Access to Energy*, a scientific newsletter, had his daughter dismissed from SOU because she refused to study its course on atheistic humanism. One year later she was readmitted following a proposed million dollar lawsuit.

131

The Cincinnati Enquirer

D4   MONDAY, SEPTEMEBER 6, 1999

Exhibit 51

1999

ABBY VAN BUREN

DEAR ABBY: After reading the letter from "Frustrated," who was looking for an alternative to a religious wedding ceremony, may I suggest secular Humanist clergy?

I am a Humanist minister from the Humanist Society of Friends whose celebrants, ministers, chaplains, counselors and pastors are all secular Humanists. You can find us throughout the United States and Canada. For details, your readers can call the American Humanist Association toll-free number: (800) 743-6646, or e-mail them at *humanism(at)juno.com.*

I have performed nonreligious weddings, funerals and naming ceremonies since 1963, when I first obtained my license from the state of Ohio to solemnize marriages. My state license is identical to that of any other clergy.

**—DR. RICK RICKARDS,
CLEVELAND**

DEAR DR. RICKARDS: Thank you for pointing this out. After I printed that letter, I was flooded with letters from readers telling me that Humanist celebrants function the same way members of traditional clergy do — with one exception: They are nontheists.

Many people also wrote to remind me that Unitarian Universalist ministers are also willing to perform ceremonies without reference to God. The telephone number of the Unitarian Universalist Association is (617) 742-2100. Their Web address is: *www.uua.org/main.html.*

To all of you who took the time to write, thank you for the input.

> " ... may I suggest secular Humanist clergy? I am a Humanist minister from the Humanist Society of Friends whose celebrants, ministers, chaplains, counselors and pastors are all secular Humanists. "

> " ... I was flooded with letters from readers telling me that Humanist celebrants function the same way members of traditional clergy do — with one exception: They are nontheists. "

That Secular Humanists provide the functions of other religions is confirmed by the words of the Humanist minister, Dr. Rick Rickards, from Cleveland, Ohio. He represents the Humanist Society of Friends and recommends the American Humanist Association for more information regarding Humanist clergy and ceremonies.

Page 1G   July 8, 2000

Atheists need fellowship, too

By Selwyn Crawford
Staff Writer of The Dallas Morning News

IRVING — When four former Catholic altar boys started an atheist "church" here a few years ago, they didn't think they were doing anything special. They just wanted a place where they and other nonbelievers could gather for fellowship, just as other churchgoers do.

But five years later, the North Texas Church for Freethought — nicknamed the "church for the unchurched" — has become a model for other atheist congregations, sparking interest in similar ventures around Texas, the nation and the world.

"It's an idea that I had for many years," said Dr. Tim Gorski, one of the four founders of the group, which is believed to be the nation's largest atheist congregation. "I had no idea it would get to be as successful as it's become."

How successful? About 40 people attended the first service in Irving's Wilson World Hotel in 1995. The church now boasts a membership of 150 and is raising money toward owning its own building.

And in March, leaders helped launch a congregation in Houston. Atheists in England and New Zealand have also contacted them about starting a church.

"We're the prototype," Dr. Gorski said proudly. "But we advertise in the newspaper. And we have an extensive Web site. And we have people who pass the word along by word of mouth."

Freethought co-founder and executive director Mike Sullivan said that although the philosophy of atheism is obviously not new, the possibility of having a "church of unbelievers" is. He said that modern-day technology is responsible for the growth and interest that the North Texas group has inspired.

"I don't think a project such as ours would have been possible without the Internet," Mr. Sullivan said, who estimated that the group gets 200 "hits" per day on its homepage (church.freethought.org). "The Internet spreads knowledge and information so quickly."

Houston's Freethought Church was formed, for example, after its organizers found the North Texas group's Web

Please see ATHEIST on Page 6G.

Page 6G   July 8, 2000

Atheist services full of familiar elements

Continued from Page 1G.

page. They say its leaders played a huge role in the development of their congregation, which follows the North Texas blueprint, down to the lunch gathering after each monthly service.

"We don't have the turnout that they have yet, but they were very instrumental for us," said co-founder and executive director Art Fay, who said services are drawing 15 to 18 people. "We wanted to use their materials because of the success they've had in five years."

Jim Ashmore, services director for the Houston organization, said the North Texas group's encouragement was critical.

"They provided the model and said that this could be done, that atheists and freethinkers could be organized into a church," Mr. Ashmore said. "I didn't believe that it could be."

Mr. Sullivan said the church offers atheists, humanists and other "freethinkers" many of the same things that theistic places of worship provide, including a disbelief in false gods. But he said atheists take that precept one big step further.

"We've rejected all other gods — plus one more," Mr. Sullivan said.

Mr Sullivan said atheists find belief in God — the God Christians, Jews and Muslims worship — unreasonable.

"The beauty of this church is that the entire world of human ideas is open to us," Mr. Sullivan said. "We are not limited by one thought or belief."

Mr. Sullivan and Dr. Gorski say understand that for many people, the idea of atheists going to "church" is a foreign concept. But they said nonbelievers share a need for fellowship.

"I think we missed church," Dr. Gorski said. "We missed the chance to get together and fellowship. Theological proositions are not like mathematical propositions, where there is only one right answer. When I though about God, I didn't have to believe one way or the other."

John Hendricks, a former Presbyterian, has attended the meetings for four years.

"It's like people that aren't religious, they still need a community to come together," Mr. Hendricks said after a recent service. "We're not a bunch of angry atheists. There are a lot of smart people here."

Freethought members come from all racial backgrounds, and Mr. Sullivan is proud that many members are younger people with families.

"We are not an organization founded on being against something," Mr. Sullivan said. "We're an organization founded on being for something — reason, tolerance and the search for truth."

Mr. Sullivan also stressed that the fellowship "is not a club" and requires no dues. The nonprofit organization does not collect offerings during services, but it does solicit and accept donations to pay the group's operating costs. According to the group's Web site, members can designate that 1 percent of their purchases at Kroger and Tom Thumb stores be donated to the church through the groceries' Kroger Cares and Good Neighbor programs.

About 75 people usually show up for the hourlong services at the hotel, or "mini-symposiums" as Dr. Gorski calls them, where topics range from ethics to behavior to current events to religion. He said that the church is always exploring avenues for various topics and that almost anything — including the Bible and God — are open for discussion.

A recent service began with a performance by two cellists, followed by a couple singing a folk song — no hymns, remember — and then a spoof on *Star Trek: The Next Generation.*

Dr. Gorski spoke to the casually dressed group about the theory of freethought, telling them, among other things, that "real freethought is thought" and that "freethinkers understand that nothing we think is beyond question." He also told them about freethought "heroes" who lived centuries ago.

Meanwhile, in a room across the hall, Dr. Gorski's wife, Deborah Boak, was instructing the children's Sunday school class.

"There are two things we try to do," Ms. Boak said "Establish critical thinking skills, and the other part is moral thinking. We probably share 90 percent of what other churches think [about right and wrong]. We believe that once you make a commitment to do what is right, you don't need a god hanging over you to force you to do it. The people here are comfortable believing you can be a good person and lead a good life."

Unlike most of the people who attend Freethought services, member Clinton Smith said that he has been an atheist since childhood.

Though his dad was a preacher, he lived in Germany with his stepdad, who was an atheist. "When you're growing up, you do what your parents do," said Mr. Smith, who has been a member of fellowship since its founding.

Mr. Smith's girlfriend, Martina Kolmeder, said that she joined the group after a long spiritual journey.

"I grew up very religious," Ms. Kolmeder said. "I tried everything. Then I read Bertrand Russell's book *Why I Am Not a Christian.* Russell's book changed my life. But it was very difficult for me to turn away [from Christianity]. People told me that if you turn away from God, you're going to hell. Now I don't worry about that."

Dr. Gorski said that he realizes that Christians' thought about freethinkers or atheists run the gamut from benign acceptance to outright contempt. He said that's fine though, because he has reciprocal feelings about most Christians. And he said that just as they ponder his fate, he wonders about theirs.

"Our question is, is it possible to know anything with absolute certainty?" Dr. Gorski asked. "As long as you're alive, nothing is ever final."

> "[T]he North Texas Church for Freethought — nicknamed the "church for the unchurched" — has become a model for other atheist congregations, sparking interest in similar ventures around Texas, the nation and the world."

Atheists have their own churches, complete with non-profit status, in Dallas and elsewhere. Yet some insist that they are not religious. Why? The main reason seems to rest in their desired access to public schools.

A World Religions Reader

SECOND EDITION

BLACKWELL
Publishers

Exhibit 53

2000

Contents

Ian S. Markham, in his book, *A World Religions Reader*, juxtaposes Secular Humanism with major world religions. While Markham defines religion as contrary to secularism, even within the second chapter he quotes Secular Humanists who claim that their worldview – Secular Humanism – is religious (though he fails to include the most explicit quotes from that document that evidence this fact).

> **Religion, for me, is a way of life (one which embraces a total world view, certain ethical demands, and certain social practices) that refuses to accept the secular view that sees human life as nothing more than comples bundles of atoms in an ultimately meaningless universe.**

Purpose and Method

After Wittgenstein the quest for all-embracing devinition that captures the essence of all forms of religion is no longer appropriate. Nevertheless a writer's attempt at a definition sets the contours for subsequent analysis. So, with modesty and for practical purposes, I offer a "definition" of religion that both underlies and embraces the descrptions that follow in this book. **Religion, for me, is a way of life (one which embraces a total world view, certain ethical demands, and certain social practices) that refuses to accept the secular view that sees human life as nothing more than comples bundles of atoms in an ultimately meaningless universe.** Positively, this definition stresses the potentially all-embracing nature of religion; negatively, it stresses the religious hostility to the modern secular world view. Not all those who call themselves "religious" would necessarily agree that religion is all-embracing, but the role-models in all traditions (Jesus, the Buddha, etc.) do set just such an ideal. And even the most anti-metaphysical form of Buddhism would concede that reductionist sciende is a distortion of the way the world is. Certainly, a textbook concentrating on the "orthodox" (i.e., traditional and widespread beliefs) strands of all traditions would accept this definition as capturing an essential element of their tradition.

Pages 5-6

Secular Humanism   43

FIRST: In the best sense, religion may inspire dedication to the highest ethical ideal. The cultivation of moral devotion and creative imagination is an expression of genuine "spiritual" experience and aspiration.

We believe, however, that traditional dogmatic or authoritarian religions that place revelation, God, ritual, or creed above human needs and experience do a disservice to the human species. Any account of nature should pass the tests of scientific evidence; in our judgment, the dogmas and myths of traditional religions do not do so. Even at this late date in human history, certain elementary facts based upon the critical use of scinetific reason have to be restated. We find insufficient evidence for belief in the existence of a supernatural; it is either meaningless or irrelevant to the question of survival and fulfillment of the human race. As nontheists, we begin with humans not God, nature not deity. Nature may indeed be broader and deeper than we now know; any new discoveries, however, will but enlarge our knowledge of the natural. . . .

We appreciate the need to preserve the best ethical teaching in the religious traditions of humankind, many of which we share in common. But we reject those features of traditional religious morality that deny humans a full appreciation of their own potentialities and responsibilities. . . .

[From the *Humanist Manifesto II*, reprinted in Markham.]

> **In the best sense, religion may inspire dedication to the highest ethical ideal. The cultivation of moral devotion and creative imagination is an expression of genuine "spiritual" experience and aspiration.**

Conclusion

CONCLUSION

Prior to World War II, Adolf Hitler re-armed Germany under the cover of deceptively-named factories. According to legend, a worker in one of Hitler's "baby buggy" factories, upon discovering that his wife was pregnant, asked a factory supervisor for a buggy. The supervisor refused, so the worker resolved to steal parts from every section of the factory until he could reassemble a buggy at home. When he finally put the parts together, however, he found something a little more dangerous than a buggy: a machine gun.

Today, America's public schools operate a lot like Hitler's "buggy" factories: they advertise "value-neutral" education, but when the student gets all the parts assembled, he finds a full-fledged worldview, a religion— Secular Humanism.

The evidence that Secular Humanism is a religion is overwhelming. But is this religion in America's public schools? Consider the "parts": values clarification, defining deviancy up,[1] "God" and "Christ" deleted from the Mayflower Compact, the loss of traditional families in literature,[2] AIDS education promoting the homosexual lifestyle, Captain Condom, Planned Parenthood, evolution without alternatives, moral relativism, multiculturalism, radical feminism, radical environmentalism, political correctness, etc.

True, most educators don't call themselves Secular Humanists. In fact, many public school teachers are committed Christians seeking to counter the Humanist influence. Many more are men and women who

141

rarely promote their own conscious agendas. Unfortunately, these educators are often thwarted by the organized minority: teachers who preach Humanistic principles—sometimes explicitly, but more often cloaked in various disguises such as "values clarification" and "academic freedom."

It doesn't matter what label these teachers assign to their agenda; Secular Humanist dogma by any other name is every bit as deadly. Teaching naturalistic evolution, spontaneous generation, ethical relativism, and legal positivism is akin to teaching the doctrines of the Secular Humanist worldview—no matter what you call it. For these educators, the mere acknowledgment of the God of the Bible is offensive on the face of it (since it directly challenges the naturalist precepts of their religion), while they freely preach what M. Stanton Evans describes as "the precepts of Darwinian-Huxleyan evolution, extreme environmentalism, the value-free 'alternative lifestyle' view of homosexuality and sexual conduct generally, and other neopaganism in their school work."[3]

"While the organized secular humanist movement," says Thomas Sowell, "might seem to be a small fringe group, its impact on education is out of all proportion to its size."[4] Part of the reason for this is that many educators adhere to Humanist dogma while calling it something else: atheism, agnosticism, skepticism, liberalism, etc.

Christians have decried this Humanist chokehold on the public schools for decades. Dr. James C. Dobson and Gary Bauer warn that this chokehold now extends to virtually every nook and cranny in our culture: "The humanistic system of values has now become the predominant way of thinking in most of the power centers of society. It has outstripped Judeo-Christian precepts in the universities, in the news media, in the entertainment industry, in the judiciary, in the federal bureaucracy, in business, medicine, law, psychology, sociology, in the arts, in many public schools and, to be sure, in the halls of Congress."[5]

Dr. Paul Vitz, a professor of psychology at New York University, was commissioned by the U.S. government to study the state of education in our public schools. He found that the Humanist bias of many educators had erased God and Christianity from the curricula, and even from history: "[A] very widespread secular and liberal mindset appears to be responsible. This mindset pervades the leadership in the world of education (and textbook publishing) and a secular and liberal bias is its inevitable consequence."[6] Vitz goes on to provide an egregious example of this bias: "Most disturbing was the constant omission of reference to the large role that religion has always played in American life. This fact has been seen as a fundamental feature of American society by foreign observers since de Tocqueville."[7]

In the past, many doubters waved away such assertions by Dobson, Bauer and Vitz as prejudices of an "intolerant" religion. Today, it is much more difficult to dismiss the reality that the Secular Humanist worldview dominates the classroom. In fact, both Christian and non-Christian scholars now frankly admit that Humanism is the only religion taught to American children in state schools.

Harvard Divinity School professor Harvey Cox recognizes Secular Humanism as "a new closed world view which functions very much like a new religion." The danger arises, says Cox, "where it pretends not to be a world view but nonetheless seeks to impose its ideology through the organs of the state."[8]

Harold Berman, a former law professor at Harvard University, says, "[In] the twentieth [century, there] has been the very gradual reduction of the traditional religions to the level of a personal, private matter, without public influence on legal development, while other belief systems—new secular religions ('ideologies,' 'isms')—have been raised to the level of passionate faiths for which people collectively are willing not only to die but also . . . to live new lives."[9]

Yale University history professor Donald Kagan characterizes the present educational landscape as follows: "[A] vulgar form of Nihilism [based upon Nietzsche's 'God is dead philosophy'[10]] has a remarkable influence in our educational system today, from elementary school through our universities. The consequences of the victory of such ideas would be enormous. If both religion and reason are removed, all that remains is will and power, where the only law is that of tooth and claw."[11]

> "We have seen that their [the public schools] complete secularization is logically inevitable. Christians must prepare themselves then, for the following results: All prayers, catechisms, and Bibles will ultimately be driven out of the schools."
> —R.L. Dabney, a 19th century Presbyterian minister

These conclusions were supported in an issue of the *Journal of Higher Education*. Dr. Howard W. Hintz writes,

But what shall we say about other kinds of dogma which are being rather extensively and insistently propounded in many courses covering the whole range of the curriculum in most of the colleges and universities which are not specifically sectarian or denominational in character? I refer, of course, to the dogma of materialism, naturalism, and scientific humanism which are being widely and unabashedly preached in my own and many other colleges both large and small, public and private. . . . And curiously enough, this type of dogmatic thinking is not only acceptable, but respectable and fashionable in college and university circles."[12]

In the same issue, Dr. Will Herberg admits that the dogma of Secular Humanism (especially, 'man is the measure of all things') "permeates" much of contemporary education.[13]

Case in point—Dr. Reed Bell. In his book, *Prescription Death: Compassionate Killers in the Medical Profession*, Dr. Bell describes a bioethics course he attended at Vanderbilt University. The course, taught by John Lachs, was entitled "Individual Rights and the Public Good in the Treatment of Humans."

On the first day of class Lachs encouraged the students to be "open-minded" about the subject matter and to expect to change their mindset about the practice of medicine. Says Bell, "The professor's ethical discourse conveyed the primary message: that we should accept as ethical—abortion, infanticide, condoned suicide, and euthanasia."[14]

"After the first week," says Dr. Bell, "I approached the professor and asked him where these new ideas came from for the practice of medicine. He handed me a copy of the *Humanist Manifesto II* and told me this was the source of the New Ethic."[15] The Bible is censored from the classroom, only to be replaced by a new "Bible": *Humanist Manifestos I, II*, and *2000*.

In their most candid moments, even Secular Humanists admit that their dogma is in the public schools (see Exhibits 8, 43, 45). Leading Secular Humanist attorney Leo Pfeffer says that if the teachings of Humanism were removed from the public schools "the consequences may be no less than the disintegration of our public school system."[16] Paul Kurtz puts it this way: "We think that the teaching of science, evolution, and humanistic values has an appropriate place in the public schools and in public life."[17]

The irony, of course, is that Humanistic thinking has free reign in the classroom because all other religions have been legally expelled. Under the present interpretation of the First Amendment, a wall of separation keeps the "church" (mostly Christianity and Judaism, along with some Buddhism, Hinduism, Islam, etc.) out of the state and state schools. The result? One religion, Humanism, becomes the unofficial "established church" of America. Americans must financially support (with their tax dollars) Humanist proselytizing in the classroom.

Imagine a child enrolled in a public school and learning only what that public school imparted (with no outside interference from family, church, Christian teachers or Congressional chaplains). When he graduated, what would he believe? Without divine intervention, he wouldn't have much choice: Secular Humanism would be all he knew.

This situation is idyllic, as far as the Humanists are concerned. Because their doctrines are every bit as dogmatic as Christian doctrine, and because they view Christianity as a "rotting corpse,"[18] they use their established position to censor any hint of positive Christian influence in the classroom. Though they posture as "open-minded," "tolerant" folks, Humanists eagerly discriminate against Christianity in the classroom.[19]

Perhaps the best example of this is the recent outrage generated by the biology textbook *Of Pandas and People* by Percival Davis and Dean H. Kenyon. Because this text acknowledges the abundance of design manifest in the natural world and thus reasonably postulates an intelligent Designer, Humanists and other non-Christians have worked themselves into a fever pitch of hysteria.

When school trustees in Plano, Texas, wanted to include *Of Pandas and People* in the public high school science curriculum, for example, Humanist educators cast aside all pretense of "tolerance." Eugenie Scott, director of the National Center for Science Education, called the text "sneaky creation science,"[20] and Frank Sonleitner, an associate professor of zoology at the University of Oklahoma, dogmatically asserted that the text was misleading because "The supernatural just doesn't have any place in the realm of science."[21] *Of Pandas and People* has already been censored by anti-Christians in various school districts in Idaho, Alabama, and California.

Prof. Phillip E. Johnson speaks to this point as follows: "When Carl Sagan and Richard Dawkins preach atheism to schoolchildren in the name of science, they are rewarded for their contributions to public education by the top scientific organizations of their respective countries. Sagan with the Public Service medal of the National Academy of Sciences and Dawkins with the Michael Faraday Award from the British Royal Society."[22]

Other award-winning scientists like Dr. Paul Davies are disqualified from teaching their views in the public schools. Why? Their beliefs controvert Humanist dogma. Davies, for example, concludes, "Having spent half a lifetime working at the forefront of fundamental physics, I have found the use of words like 'design' 'meaning' and 'purpose' irresistible."[23] Such concepts will not be allowed in the public school system of America because they compete with the religious dogma of Secular Humanism.

The consequences of this unofficial establishment of Secular Humanism as the "state religion" have been disastrous. Truth has been undermined, academic freedom has suffered, and—most importantly— many unprepared students have "converted" to a godless religion. Even students who are able to hold fast to their Christianity in these anti-Christian environments see their values attacked daily.

If you believe in special creation, you'll be mocked in biology class. If you believe America was founded according to Christian principles, you'll be mocked in history class. And woe to the student who still holds biblical beliefs about sex and family!

The public schools, under the guise of Project 10, the Rainbow Curriculum, healthy "sex education" and even "multiculturalism" continue to promote the homosexual lifestyle as an innocent, biologically-determined alternate lifestyle. The National Education Association is presently promoting a manual for training educators on issues involving "gay and lesbian students" and recommending that the word "marriage" be replaced with "permanent relationships."

Says Peter LaBarbera, "The NEA 'Handbook for Educators' contains advice from a host of pro-homosexual school-oriented programs across the country—from Project 10 in Los Angeles to the Harvey Milk school for homosexual youth in New York City." The 'Handbook' advises stocking school libraries with books promoting 'sexual diversity,' ridding libraries of 'pejorative' books on homosexuality, conducting gay-affirming 'sensitivity' training for students, teachers and administrators, changing 'heterosexist language,' and introducing 'gay/lesbian issues into all curriculum areas.'[24]

Some students from Christian homes are prepared to withstand such attacks on their faith and values; others are eventually swayed by the constant assault. The heartache suffered by the parents of these "Humanist converts" is best summed up in a letter from a mother in Salem, Oregon.

"Our daughter," she writes, "was raised in Christian schools and in a

Christian home where we taught her Christian values and morals and she learned that Jesus Christ is the way of salvation. Two years out of high school at 20 years old she enrolled at the University of Oregon. We were apprehensive but trusted her judgement as she had always shown clear vision. We did not know this is one of the most liberal [Humanistic] universities in the nation. Unfortunately she was overwhelmed by the professors and began to believe their [Humanistic] philosophies. She graduated two years ago with a political science and English degree and has turned her back on all that she believed in. We are trusting God to bring our girl back. The wait is sometimes difficult, but we are on bended knee."

Faith does not give way to lack of faith—it instead is replaced by a competing faith. In this case, a young lady's faith in God was replaced by what John Dewey would call the "common faith"—faith in "man is the measure of all things," which translates into selfishness, godlessness, spontaneous generation, evolution and moral relativism.

Such a situation is not "fair" in any sense of the word. Surely the most basic role of the state—promoting justice (Romans 13:1-4)—requires the state to treat citizens fairly, rather than forcing one religion on every citizen.

As William Jennings Bryan says, "[I]n schools supported by taxation we should have a real neutrality wherever neutrality in religion is desired. If the Bible cannot be defended in these schools it should not be attacked, either directly or under the guise of philosophy or science. The neutrality which we now have is often but a sham; it carefully excludes the Christian religion but permits the use of the schoolroom for the destruction of faith and for the teaching of materialistic doctrines."[25]

Historian George M. Marsden agrees with Bryan's observation and says, "Bryan here correctly identified a major problem in American democracy. If Christianity was no longer going to be the established religion, either officially or unofficially, in the tax-supported schools, then what philosophy would be established? If doctrines of materialism prevailed and schools routinely taught that all religion was an illusory human creation, then irreligion would be established. Darwin's own version of Darwinism was materialistic and philosophies built on evolutionary analogies increasingly were given a materialistic bent. Such philosophies, whatever their merits, Bryan was pointing out, should hardly be permitted to travel under the colors of neutrality toward religion."[26]

This unfairness is especially noteworthy in biology courses, where evolution is presented as indisputable fact. If the public schools were truly interested in presenting a balanced education, says Dr. Duane Gish, "the scientific evidences which support creation [would] be taught along with the scientific evidences which support evolution. . . ."[27] Instead, any hint of design in today's biology classes is described as a "fundamentalist" effort to replace science with religion. Such a double standard is not fair. This unofficial

Figure 1.

The Religious Equality Amendment

Resolved by the Senate and the House of Representatives of the United States of America in Congress Assembled (two-thirds of the House concuring therein), that the following article is proposed as an amendment to the Constitution of the United States, which shall be valid to all intents and purposes as part of the Constitution when ratified by the legislatures of three-fourths of the several States within seven years after the date of its submission for ratification.

In order to secure the unalienable right of the people to acknowledge God according to the dictates of conscience;

Section I. Neither the United States not any State shall abridge the freedom of any person or group, including students in public schools, to engage in prayer or other religious expression in circumstances in which expression of a non-religious character would be permitted, nor deny benefits to or otherwise discriminate against any person or group on account of the religious character of their speech, ideas, motivations, or identity.

Section II. Nothing in the Constitution shall be construed to forbid the United States or any State to give public or ceremonial acknowledgement to the religious heritage, beliefs, or traditions of its people.

Section III. The exercise, by the people, of any freedoms under the First Amendment or under this Amendment shall not constitute an establishment of religion.*

*The precise wording of the Religious Equality Amendment is still being honed and may be slightly different in its final form. There are continuing negotiations in regard to the exact wording of Section II.

establishment of a tax-supported "state religion" is exactly the type of tyranny America's founding fathers sought to avoid.

How can we reclaim this lost ground?

Some Christians answer this question by asking another: Why is the government involved in education in the first place? A strong case can be made for the belief that God expects the family to train our children (Proverbs 22:6), and that the state is overstepping its jurisdiction when it attempts to educate.[28] If parents accepted the responsibility assigned to them by God, according to this perspective, we'd have no need for state-controlled public schools.

It is not the purpose of this book to critique this argument. We leave the reader to draw his own conclusions, while we address a more urgent question: As long as public schools exist, what can be done about the Secular Humanist monopoly in those classrooms?

The first step, we believe, requires acknowledging a basic truth: value-neutral education is a myth. Since every thinking individual adheres to some worldview, and since every worldview proposes values that motivate the adherent, no teacher can completely separate his values from the content of his teaching. Just as a committed Christian would be unwilling to deceive his students by presenting abortion as an acceptable form of birth control, so also a Marxist would be unwilling to "deceive" his students by describing capitalism as an acceptable economic system. Good teachers won't deceive their students; thus, they allow their worldviews to shape the content of their presentations.

When we recognize this value-neutral hoax, we should simultaneously realize the basic unfairness of a policy that bans only those religions with explicitly absolute values from the classroom. Instead of discriminating against Christianity and other traditional religions, the government should open the doors and allow knowledgeable proponents of both theistic and atheistic worldviews in the public schools, in the courts, and in the various government agencies. Such a policy, though imperfect, at least allows the U.S. government to establish an even-handed approach with regard to religions.[29]

Put simply, if Dr. Carl Sagan can show his "Cosmos" series in the public schools, then creationist Dr. A.E. Wilder-Smith's "Origins" must be allowed.

If ethical relativism can be taught, then ethical absolutes must be given their day in court, too. Captain Condom's "safe sex" message should be countered by the Family Research Council's "Virtuous Reality"—abstinence.

149

If positive law is taught, then time must be given for natural law. If socialism and the welfare state are presented, then the free market and private property must have their say, too. If Western civilization is denounced, then equal time must be given to describe the triumphs of Western civilization.[30]

> "The competitions of the State and Church for power over education have been so engrossing that we have almost forgotten the parent, the third and rightful competitor."
> —R.L. Dabney

Another noteworthy effort to disband the Humanist monopoly in the classroom has been spearheaded by a coalition of Christian organizations (including the Family Research Council, American Family Association, and Focus on the Family). With an eye toward protecting Christian students' rights to free speech and assembly in the public schools, this coalition is championing a "Religious Equality Amendment" to the U.S. Constitution (See Figure 1). This amendment would represent an important step toward upsetting the status quo secularism in the public schools.

Until this Humanist monopoly is shattered, many parents will find themselves in the same predicament as the mother in Oregon who "lost" her daughter. The wise family must take every precaution to guard against the Humanist clergy in the classroom.

One of the very best precautions, we believe, involves training students to "take every thought captive for Christ" (2 Corinthians 10:5) at a Summit Ministries Christian Leadership Seminar. Such training has, by the grace of God, led to many success stories and many encouraging letters, including the following letter from a three-time seminar graduate: "As a former Summit student and excellence program graduate, I always enjoy playing guerilla warfare with my professors, or as Martin Anderson would say, 'Impostors in the Temple.' I attend Columbia University in the city of New York. . . . You'll also be happy to know that I am presently working with other Christians to produce 'The Columbia Standard,' a Christian newspaper."[31]

C.S. Lewis's description of Christians as soldiers dropped behind enemy lines holds true in every age—but never more so than today. The peculiar tragedy of modern America is that our "soldiers" in the deepest regions of hostile territory are our children—a new generation fighting battles with the very adults pretending to train them up in the way they should go. To correct this grievous situation, Christian adults must reclaim this territory and assume responsibility for providing an alternative education. Instead of placing our children on the front lines, we must face the fiercest fighting ourselves. The price will be dear, but our reward—the hearts and minds of our children—is incomparable.

NOTES

1. "In any society or culture when 'the deviant is declared normal and the normal is unmasked as deviant' vast changes are underway." Paul Hollander, *Anti-Americanism: Irrational and Rational* (New Brunswick, NJ: Transaction Publishers, 1995), p. xxiii. Also see Charles Krauthammer, "Defining Deviancy Up" in *New Republic*, Nov. 22, 1993, and Daniel Patrick Moynihan, "Defining Deviancy Down" in *American Scholar*, Winter 1993.

2. "Public school textbooks commonly exclude the history, heritage, beliefs, and values of millions of Americans. Those who believe in the traditional family are not represented. Over and over, we have seen that liberal and secular bias is primarily accomplished by exclusion, by leaving out the opposing position. Such a bias is harder to observe than a positive vilification or direct criticism, but it is the essence of censorship." Dr. Paul C. Vitz, quoted in Paul Hollander, *Anti-Americanism*, p. 196.

3. M. Stanton Evans, *The Theme is Freedom: Religion, Politics and the American Tradition* (Washington, DC: Regnery Publishing, Inc., 1994), p. 129.

4. Thomas Sowell, *Inside American Education* (New York: Macmillan Free Press, 1993), p. 59.

5. James C. Dobson and Gary L. Bauer, *Children At Risk* (Dallas, TX: Word Publishing, 1990), p. 22.

6. Paul C. Vitz, *Censorship: Evidence of Bias in Our Children's Textbooks* (Ann Arbor, MI: Servant Books, 1986), p. 1.

7. Ibid., pp. 2-3.

8. Harvey Cox, *The Secular City: Secularization and Urbanization in Theological Perspective*, rev. ed. (New York: Macmillan, 1965, 1966), p. 18.

9. Harold Berman, *The Interaction of Law and Religion* (1974), quoted in John W. Whitehead and John Conlan, "The Establishment of the Religion of Secular Humanism and Its First Amendment Implications," *Texas Tech Law Review* 10, no. 1 (1978): 32.

10. "Nihilism rejects any objective basis for society and its morality, the very concept of objectivity, even the possibility of communication itself." Donald Kagan, *Academic Questions* 8, no. 2 (spring 1995): 56.

11. Ibid.

12. *Journal of Higher Education* 23 (October 1952): 361-62.

13. Ibid., p. 366.

14. Reed Bell and Frank York, *Prescription Death: Compassionate Killers in the Medical Profession* (Lafayette, LA: Huntington House Publishers, 1993), p. 41.

15. Ibid.

16. *The Humanist*, September/October 1988, p. 50.

17. *Free Inquiry* 11, no. 4 (Fall 1991): 50.

18. See John Dunphy, "A Religion for a New Age," *The Humanist* (January/February 1983): 26.

19. Example after example of this Christophobia is contained in James Dobson, "Focus on the Family Newsletter," May 1995.

20. Quoted in Alexei Barrionuevo, "Science Book Creating Dissent," *The Dallas Morning News*, Jan. 12, 1995, p. 24A.

21. Ibid.

22. *Christianity Today*, February 6, 1995, p. 12.

23. *The Washington Times*, March 9, 1995, p. A6.

24. Peter LaBarbera, "NEA Zealously Promotes Gay Agenda," in *Human Events*, March 31, 1995, p. 7.

25. George M. Marsden, *The Soul of the American University* (New York: Oxford University Press, 1994), p. 326.

26. Ibid.

27. Duane Gish, "The Nature of Science and of Theories of Origins," *Impact*, April 1995, p. 4.

28. See Robert Thoburn, *The Children Trap* (Ft. Worth, TX: Dominion Press, 1986).

29. A still greater measure of freedom could be provided if the Government allowed parents to choose the public school that their children will attend. In this way, parents would be free to choose the school that educates according to their own worldview. Humanists could send their children to Humanist-dominated schools, and Christians to Christian-dominated schools. The most effective means for establishing this freedom involves tax credits, whereby families with school-age children receive a tax break and can apply the money saved to the tuition of any school they choose. For an in-depth discussion of this option, see Rockne McCarthy, et al., *Society, State, and Schools* (Grand Rapids, MI: William B. Eerdmans Publishing, 1981), pp. 170-174.

30. Yale professor Donald Kagan insists that college freshmen make the study of Western civilization the center of their pursuit of a liberal education. He notes that the United States is a nation that depends on a set of beliefs and

institutions deriving from Western traditions. He says, "I argued that the unity of our country and the defense of its political freedom and individual liberties required that its citizens have a good understanding of the ideas, history and traditions that created them." *Academic Questions* 8, no.2 (spring 1995): 51.

31. Another effective method to prepare students to stand firm against Humanist indoctrination involves close study of the worldview analysis text by David A. Noebel, *Understanding the Times: The Religious Worldviews of Our Day and the Search for Truth* (Eugene, OR: Harvest House, 1994).

RECOMMENDED READING

Anderson, Martin. *Impostors in the Temple: American Intellectuals are Destroying our Universities and Cheating Our Students of their Future.* New York: Simon and Schuster, 1992.

Beckwith, Francis J. *Rethinking Edwards v. Aguillard?: The Establishment Clause of the First Amendment and the Challenge of Intelligent Design.* Master of Juridical Studies Thesis. St. Louis, MO: Washington University School of Law, 2001.

Bernstein, Richard. *Dictatorship of Virtue.* New York: Alfred A. Knopf, 1994.

Collier, Peter, and David Horowitz. *Destructive Generation.* Lenham, MD: Second Thoughts Books, 1991.

D'Souza, Dinesh. *Illiberal Education.* New York: The Free Press, 1991.

Dobson, James C., and Gary L. Bauer. *Children at Risk.* Dallas, TX: Word Publishing, 1990.

Hand, Judge W. Brevard. *American Education on Trial: Is Secular Humanism a Religion?* Cumberland, VA: Center for Judicial Studies, 1987.

House, H. Wayne. "A Tale of Two Kingdoms: Can There Be a Peaceable Co-existence of Religion with the Secular State." *BYU Journal of Public Law* 13:2 (1999): 203ff.

House, H. Wayne. "Darwinism and the Law: Can Non-Naturalistic Scientific Theories Survive Constitutional Challenge?" *Regent University Law Review*, 13:2 (2000-2001): 355-445.

Hunter, James Davison, and Os Guiness, eds. *Articles of Faith, Articles of Peace: The Religious Liberty Clauses and the American Public Philosophy.* Washington, D.C.: The Bookings Institution, 1990.

Kilpatrick, William. *Why Johnny Can't Tell Right from Wrong.* New York: Simon and Schuster, 1992.

Kimball, Roger. *Tenured Radicals.* New York: Harper and Row, 1990.

LaHaye, Tim, and David A. Noebel. *Mind Siege.* Nashville, TN: Word, 2001.

Marsden, George M. *The Soul of the American University.* New York: Oxford Press, 1994.

Nash, Ronald H. *The Closing of American Heart: What's Really Wrong With America's Schools.* Dallas, TX: Probe Books/Distributed by Word Publishing, 1990.

Noebel, David A. *Understanding the Times: The Religious Worldviews of Our Day and the Search for Truth.* Eugene, OR: Harvest House, 1994.

Plantinga, Alvin. "Creation and Evolution: A Modest Proposal." Paper delivered at the Eastern Division Meeting of the American Philosophical Association. Washington, D.C.: American Philosophical Association, 27-30 December 1998.

Plantinga, Alvin. "Methodological Naturalism: Part 1." *Origins & Design* (Winter 1997) 18:1. http://www.arn.org/docs/odesign/od181/methnat181.htm.

Plantinga, Alvin. "Methodological Naturalism: Part 2." *Origins & Design* (Fall 1997) 18:2. http://www.arn.org/docs/odesign/od182/methnat182.htm.

Schlafly, Phyllis. *Child Abuse in the Classroom.* Alton, IL: Pere Marquette Press, 1984.

Sowell, Thomas. *Inside American Education: The Decline, The Deception, The Dogma.* New York: MacMillan, 1993.

Vitz, Paul A. *Censorship: Evidence of Bias in our Children's Textbooks.* Ann Arbor, MI: Servant Books, 1986.

Champions of the Christian Worldview

Summit Ministries exists to train servant leaders in worldview analysis, to equip them to champion the Christian faith, and to inspire them to love God with their hearts and mings. Since 1962, Summit Ministries has admonished Christians to avoid being captured by the so-called "wisdom" of the world (Colossians 2:8), and encouraged them to make every thought captive to Christ (2 Corinthians 10:5). Summit Ministries accomplishes this through the following programs and materials:

Understanding the Times: The definitive resource for worldview analysis, this 912-page textbook compares and contrasts Christianity, Secular Humanism, Marxist/Leninism, and the New Age movement. Also available in a 400-page abridged edition.

Summer Christian Leadership Seminars: This life-changing two week program teaches young people to understand and champion the truth of Christianity. During this academic camp, young people ages 16 and up learn how to defend their faith and live life with meaning and purpose.

Understanding the Times Curriculum: With over 70 video segments, this year-long (two semesters), comprehensive curriculum package provides all the material needed to teach your Christian high school, homeschool, church or Bible study group to understand the times and know what their country ought to do (1 Chronicles 12:32).

Lightbearer's Christian Worldview Curriculum: This video-based, two-semester-long curriculum package is designed for students in 7th-9th grades. With an emphasis upon developing their Christian worldview, this curriculum contrast the Christian perspective with the Humanist perspective. This is a self-contained curriculum containing readings, Bible memory, community and classroom projects, and tests

Worldviews in Focus – Thinking Like a Christian: This curriculum (not video-based) supplies a 12-week survey of the Biblical Christian Worldview designed for Sunday school classes, small group Bible studies, and homeschool groups.

The *Journal*: This monthly publication provides the best "review of the news" available for Christians who don't have the time to monitor all the media.

Summit Bookhouse: The Bookhouse offers one of the best collections of thoughtful worldview-oriented books available in the Christian community. The carefully selected titles cover New Age, education, economics, environmental concerns, creation and evolution, church and state, apologetics, abortion, and more.

For more information, contact us:
Summit Ministries
PO Box 207 • Manitou Springs, CO 80829
Voice (719) 685-9103 • Fax (719) 685-5268 • info@summit.org
www.summit.org